MANCHESTER
FOOTBALL TR
Volume 1 1990 - 2003

Written and researched by Mark Williams

Published by RINGWAY PUBLICATIONS
www.ringwaypublications.com

RINGWAY PUBLICATIONS

First published in Great Britain 2015

A catalogue record of this book is available from the British Library

ISBN No 978-0-9570826-7-0

Printed and bound in Great Britain by:
Crossprint Ltd
21 Barry Way
Newport Business Park
Newport
Isle of Wight
PO30 5GY
www.crossprint.co.uk

CONTENTS

COVER PHOTOGRAPH CREDITS:

Front Cover
9th June 1996 – Czech Republic fans are posing for the camera, having just arrived in Manchester aboard LET-401 OK-WDO (Michael Oldham)

Back Cover
28th May 2003 – Blue Panorama B.737-400 EI-CUN is one of over 400 extra movements in connection with the Champions League final. (Lloyd Robinson)

ACKNOWLEDGEMENTS

I would like to thank those below for their assistance, without which this book would not be possible.

MANCHESTER AIRPORT ARCHIVE

For arranging access to their archives since 1994.

Special thanks go to Michael Hancock, Business Records Officer, for his helpfulness since 2007.

PHOTOGRAPH CREDITS
(In alphabetical order)

Thanks to Geoff Ball, Lee Collins, Nik French, Peter Hampson, Ian Hawkridge, Allan Jones, Denis Norman, Michael Oldham, Stuart Prince, Lloyd Robinson, Paul Rowland, Terry Shone, Barry Swann, Rick Ward, Glenn Wheeler and Mark White for use of their wonderful images.

PROOF READER

Thanks to Martin Dennett for his diligence.

CONTRIBUTORS

My sincerest thanks go to Geoff Ball, Lloyd Robinson, Nik French, Glenn Wheeler, Chris Mann and Michael Oldham. I would also like to thank Chris Walkden for his monthly movement reports.

For reference/research, I would also like to thank TAS, Air-Britain, North West Air News and The Aviation Hobby Shop.

WEBSITE VISITORS & CONTRIBUTORS

I would also like to thank all our website visitors, from the UK and the rest of the world, especially those who have shared their memories and photographs.

Mark Williams

INTRODUCTION BY MARK WILLIAMS

Far removed from the big money teams and mass corporate sponsorship of today, where all of Europe's biggest teams meet in the UEFA Europa Champions League, the roots of European football can be traced as far back as 1909 when West Auckland FC from the North East competed in the Sir Thomas Lipton trophy which featured eight teams from across Europe. They managed to beat Swiss side FC Winterthur 2-0 in the final played on 12th April 1909, a feat that they repeated two years later.

In April 1955, UEFA established the European Cup, a football competition for the champion clubs of UEFA affiliated nations, to begin in the 1955-1956 season. However, the English League winners, Chelsea, were denied entry by the Football League, who believed it was in the best interests of English football and football in general for them not to enter. Scottish side Hibernian became the United Kingdom's entry into this inaugural, invitation-only, competition and reached the semi-finals before being knocked out by Reims. The final was played between Milan and Real Madrid on 1st May 1956, where the Spanish side won the first of their nine European Cup successes to date. It is also worth noting that Real Madrid won the trophy five times in succession from 1956-1960. The following season, the English League was won by Manchester United, managed by Matt Busby. Originally, the Football League again denied any English club entry to the European Cup but Busby and his chairman, with help of the Football Association's chairman Stanley Rous, defied the league and Manchester United became the first English team to venture into Europe. Further competitions were added, the Cup Winners' Cup in 1960 and the UEFA Cup in 1971.

The Manchester United management had taken a chance, and it had paid off, with the team – known as the "Busby Babes" for their youth – proving the Football League wrong by reaching the semi-finals of the 1956–57 competition, being knocked out by eventual winners Real Madrid. Winning the First Division title again that season meant that they secured qualification for the 1957–58 tournament, and their successful cup run in 1956–57 meant that they were one of the favourites to win it. Domestic League matches were played on Saturdays and European matches were played midweek, so although air travel was risky at the time, it was the only practical choice if United were to fulfil their league fixtures, which they would have to do.

After overcoming Shamrock Rovers and Dukla Prague in the preliminary round and the first round respectively, Manchester United were drawn with Red Star Belgrade of Yugoslavia for the quarter-finals. After beating the Yugoslavians 2–1 at Old Trafford on 21st January 1958, the club was scheduled to travel to Yugoslavia for the return leg on 5th February. On the way back from Prague in the previous round, fog over England prevented the team from flying back to Manchester, so they hastily made arrangements to fly to Amsterdam before taking the ferry from the Hook of Holland to Harwich and then the train up to Manchester. The trip took its toll on the players and they were only able to scrape a 3–3 draw with Birmingham City at St Andrew's three days later.

Eager not to miss any of their Football League fixtures in the future, and also not to have to go through such a difficult trip again, the club chartered Airspeed Ambassador G-

ALZU from British European Airways to fly the team and local press from Manchester to Belgrade for the away leg against Red Star. The match itself was drawn 3–3, but it was enough to send United to the semi-finals. The take off from Belgrade was delayed for an hour as United's outside right, Johnny Berry, had lost his passport, and then the plane made a planned stop in Munich to refuel, landing at 13:15 GMT. After two aborted attempts to depart for various reasons, the third attempt proved fatal. The plane skidded off the end of the runway, and out of control, it crashed into the fence surrounding the airport and then across a road before its port wing was torn off as it caught a house. Part of the plane's tail was torn off too, before the left side of the cockpit hit a tree. The right side of the fuselage hit a wooden hut, inside of which was a truck filled with tyres and fuel which exploded. Twenty passengers died onboard, and there were three subsequent deaths.

Despite this fatal accident, flying proved to be the only acceptable form of transport for teams to compete across Europe. Local teams playing European football in the 1960s were Manchester United (1963/64, 1964/65, 1965/66, 1967/68 & 1968/69) and a resurgent Manchester City (1968/69 & 1970), which provided numerous football charters bringing teams to Manchester. However, these matches did not always produce a mass exodus of fans to the region, due to the cost and travel restrictions involved. The culmination of this was that Manchester United won the European Cup in 1968 and Manchester City won the Cup Winners' Cup in 1970.

The following decade saw both teams competing in various European competitions without any success, but by 1985 there was worse to come. Liverpool, who by now were the major UK force in European football, had reached another European Cup Final, this time against Juventus at the Heysel Stadium in Brussels on 29th May 1985. Approximately one hour before the kick off, a large group of football hooligans breached a fence separating them from a "neutral area" which contained rival Juventus fans. The Juventus fans ran back on the terraces and away from the threat into a concrete retaining wall. Fans already seated near the wall were crushed and the wall eventually collapsed. Many people climbed over to safety, but several others were killed or badly injured. The game was played despite the disaster in order to prevent further violence. The tragedy resulted in all English football clubs being placed under an indefinite ban by UEFA from all European competitions (which was lifted in 1990–91), with Liverpool being excluded for an additional year. Fourteen Liverpool fans found guilty of involuntary manslaughter were each sentenced to three years' imprisonment. Thirty-three Juventus fans and six Liverpool fans died, and six hundred were injured. The disaster was described as "the darkest hour in the history of the UEFA competitions".

Ironically in 1990, thirty-four years after Manchester United became the first English team to play in one of the UEFA competitions, they became one of two teams, with the other being Aston Villa, to compete in Europe again. This was due to winning the FA Cup Final in May 1990, beating Crystal Palace 4-2.

This book covers the football related flights that arrived into Manchester during the period 1990-2003 and the teams connected with them.

SEASON 1990/1991
Manchester United UEFA Cup Winners' Cup

In October 1990, European football returned to England for the first time in five years following the ban on English teams after the Heysel Stadium disaster in 1985. The irony was not lost on the fact that it would be Manchester United, the first English team to win a European title, to get the ball rolling again. The Reds had qualified for the UEFA Cup Winners' Cup, having beaten Crystal Palace in the FA Cup final in May. Amazingly, they made it all the way to the final the following May, and in a nail biting final, they overcame the Spanish giants, Barcelona, 2-1 at the Feyenoord stadium in Rotterdam. United were 2-0 up with ten minutes to go, but Barcelona pulled a goal back that led to a tense and nervous ending, but the Reds managed to hang on. Interestingly, of the four European clubs that United encountered on the way to the final, Hungarian side Pecsi Mecsek, Wrexham, Montpellier and Legia Warsaw, the only team to provide any fans' charters was the French side.

Montpelier was also the only side during this campaign to fly direct into Manchester, aboard Air Littoral ATR-42 F-GEGD. It is assumed that the other teams arrived via scheduled flights, with the exception of course of Wrexham, who would have travelled in their masses down the M56 from North Wales. Travelling fans, with the exception of Montpellier and Wrexham, could be assumed to be virtually non-existent.

5ᵗʰ March 1991 – Air Littoral ATR-42 F-GEGD (LIT126 from Montpelier) arrived at 1121 with the Montpelier team officials for the following evening's match with Manchester United. The airline's ATR-42s could occasionally be seen on their scheduled flights out of Manchester. They first began regular services in April 1990, when they inaugurated a weekday Embraer EMB-120 service to Lyon and Bordeaux. Flights were extended to cover Nice, Paris-CDG and Strasbourg from May 1991, but these only lasted until the end of that summer. Bordeaux was dropped in October 1993, which just left flights to Lyon, which continued until October 1996. (Peter Hampson)

6th March 1991 – F-GIDO seen here (LIT228 from Toulouse), was the first of two Air Littoral Fokker 100s that arrived today, with Montpellier fans for their quarter-final match with Manchester United. Also arriving for today's match was TEA France B.737-300 F-GKTB (TFR091 from Montpellier), Citation 550 F-GGGT (from/to Chambery) and Beech 100 F-GJJJ (CLG331 from/to Caen). (Denis Norman)

6th March 1991 – F-GIDM was the second Air Littoral Fokker 100 today, bringing more French fans. In 1990, the airline leased six KLM Fokker 100s until 1992, when they standardised their fleet around their Embraer EMB-120s, ATR-42 & ATR-72s. (Nik French)

13ᵗʰ May 1991 - Two days ahead of the European Cup Final, Manchester United flew out to Rotterdam onboard Airtours Boeing 767-300 G-SJMC (AIH827 seen above) along with the first fans' charter, Transavia B.737-300 PH-HVK, which operated two flights out to Amsterdam. Realising that some kit had been left behind at Manchester, Northern Executive Aviation Beech 100 G-BBVM flew out to Rotterdam later the same day. (Barry Swann)

14ᵗʰ May 1991 - The mass airlift of Manchester United fans out to Amsterdam and Rotterdam began in earnest today. The following aircraft all departed between 0910 and 1630: Air Kilroe Jetstream 31 G-OAKC and Beech 200s G-OAKL & G-OAKM, Britannia Airways B.737 G-AVRN (BAL882A) and B.767-200s G-BNCW (BAL887A) & G-BOPB (BAL881A), Caledonian L.1011s G-BBAF (CKT7292) & G-BBAH (CKT7294), Dan-Air B.727 G-BPNY (UKL9265), Loganair BAe.146 G-OLCA, Monarch A.300 G-MONR (MON2044), B.737-300 G-MONV (MON1152) and B.757s G-MONE (MON2030) & G-MONK (MON2052), PA-31 Navajos G-HBCO & G-OJUG, Beech 200 G-WILK, Martinair A.310-203 PH-MCB. The final departure was Britannia Airways B.767 G-BRIF (AHD2028), on lease to Air Holland

16ᵗʰ May 1991 - The majority of the jubilant United fans returned in the early hours today on the following flights: Air Kilroe Beech 200 G-OAKM & Jetstream 31 G-OAKC, Britannia Airways B.767 G-BNCW (BAL887B), Caledonian L.1011 G-BBAH (CKT7295), Loganair BAe.146s G-OLCA (LOG838) & G-OLCB (LOG836), Monarch B.737-300 G-MONV (MON1153) and B.757s G-MONE (MON2031) & G-MONK (MON2053), Beech 200 G-WILK, PA-23 Aztec G-OANT, PA-28 Cherokee G-AVSA, PA-31 Navajos G-HBCO & G-OJUG, Beech 200 OY-PEB, Citation 500 OY-CGO, Martinair A.310 PH-MCB (MPH3133), Air Holland B.757 PH-AHN (UKL9266) on a first visit and B.767 G-BRIF (AHD2027) plus Transavia B.737-300s PH-HVG (TRA6589) & PH-HVV (TRA6857). This glorious victory on an unforgettable evening earned them an automatic place in the Cup Winners' Cup next season.

16th May 1991 - Having been victorious in Holland, the Manchester United team returned aboard another Airtours aircraft, MD-83 G-TTPT, which arrived at 1827 (AIH830 from Rotterdam). The majority of fans returned in the early hours of the 16th. In the early days of Manchester United's return to Europe, they would regularly travel to matches on UK charter airlines such as Airtours, Air 2000, Britannia and Monarch, before changing to Star Europe in the mid 1990s. (Barry Swann)

16th May 1991 – Also involved in the airlift, was Martinair A.310 PH-MCB (MPH3133 f/Amsterdam). They operated two Airbus A.310s, PH-MCA/MCB, from 1984-1994, and were regulars to Manchester on charters and sub-charters. (Peter Hampson)

SEASON 1991/1992
Manchester United UEFA Cup Winners' Cup

Fresh from winning their first European trophy since 1968, and finishing a modest sixth in the First Division, hopes must have been relatively high that this season would be another successful one for Manchester United. However, this proved not to be the case! Despite winning the League Cup for the first time in their history, they were spectacularly knocked out at the second round stage of the European Cup Winners' Cup. Further disappointment would come later in the season, when having led the First Division for much of the season; they lost out to their rivals Leeds United.

5ᵗʰ November 1991 - Air Europa B.757 EC-FEE arrived at 1126 (AE012/3) with the Athletico Madrid team and a number of fans. Another Air Europa B.757, EC-FEF (AEA014/5), arrived the following evening to pick up the victorious Spanish team after the match. The Spanish airline regularly operated football charters up until 2008. (Barry Swann)

The Reds' first European match was away to the Greek side, Athinaikos, in the first round of the Cup Winners' Cup. The actual match took place on the 18ᵗʰ September, with the team and a few fans travelling out to Athens aboard Airtours MD-83 G-TTPT (AIH887) the day earlier. The match itself was a 0-0 draw, which was followed two weeks later by the home leg at Old Trafford. There were no Greek charter flights on this occasion and the team seemingly travelled to/from Manchester via scheduled flights. Maybe this lack of support made sure they were beaten by Manchester United 2-0. The following round they were given a severe lesson in European football and tactics at the hands of Athletico Madrid. On the 22ⁿᵈ October 1991, the team flew out to Madrid on Britannia Airways

8

B.737 G-BJCU (BAL888A), with the fans travelling on the match day itself (23rd October) using the following aircraft: Britannia Airways B.737 G-AWSY (BAL890A), Monarch Airlines B.737-300 G-MONV (MON2266) and UK Leisure B.737-400 G-UKLA (UKL9457). The Spanish side were too strong for Manchester United and won easily 3-0 and the return leg on the 6th November proved to be a frustrating night. Having to score at least four goals, the Reds were constantly up against eleven Athletico players behind the ball, making it difficult for United to create any goal scoring opportunities. In the end, the match ended 1-1; the Spanish side got what they came for, a favourable result and the dumping of Manchester United out of the competition.

SEASON 1992/1993
Manchester United UEFA Cup

Cup competitions for Manchester United this season were very disappointing. As holders, they were knocked out in the third round of the League Cup by Aston Villas, and in the fifth round of the FA Cup to Sheffield United. They fared even worse in the first round of the UEFA Cup. Drawn against Torpedo Moscow, the first leg would be played at Old Trafford on 16th September. The team and officials had arrived the day earlier on Aeroflot Tupolev TU-134 CCCP-65781 (AFL1249/50 f/t Moscow). There should have been a couple of fans' charters from Moscow, but their applications for visas were granted too late for the flights to be arranged. The match itself was made difficult by a Russian block of players in front of them throughout the ninety minutes, resulting in a disappointing 0-0 draw. The away was played on 29th September, with Manchester United flying out two days earlier on British Midland DC-9 G-ELDG (BMA8271). This match also ended in a 0-0 draw, which led to a penalty shoot out. With the penalties standing at 4-3 to the Russian side, Gary Pallister had to score his penalty to keep the game alive, but unfortunately it was saved and the Reds were out of Europe in the opening round. However, there was some consolation for United the following May, when they won the inaugural Premier League title, formerly the First Division, by a massive ten points.

11th November 1992 – Having exited the European stage two months earlier, Manchester United arranged a friendly with Norwegian side Brondby, who arrived aboard Sterling B.727 OY-SBF (SAW2993/4 from/to Copenhagen), seen here on short finals on a dull day. The match was played the same day, which United won 3-2. Boeing 727-2J4 OY-SBF was purchased new in March 1980 by Sterling Airways, later Sterling European, until 1994. In 2014 it is based in Thailand, operating as a freighter aircraft for K-Mile Air as HS-SCK. (Paul Rowland)

SEASON 1993/1994
Manchester United UEFA Champions League
Anglo-Italian Cup (Oldham & Stoke)

The Anglo-Italian competition first began in 1970 and continued intermittently until 1996. As the title suggests, matches were played between English and Italian sides. During its time the tournament had a reputation for violence between fans, and was temporarily abolished in 1986. It was re-established in 1992, and for the start of this season's competition the system had been revised to two groups of eight teams, four from each country. Local sides Bolton Wanderers and Stoke City would compete in the competition, each playing four different Italian sides, two at home and two away. On the 11th October, Italian airline Fortune made their first visit to Manchester with DC-9-15 I-TIAN, bringing in Ancona for a match with Bolton Wanderers. The aircraft arrived from Birmingham, having dropped off another Italian side, Pescara, who were due to play West Brom the following evening.

14th September 1993 – For their match with Kispet Honved, Manx Airlines BAe.146 G-MIMA (MNX911) was used by the Manchester United team and officials for their flight to Budapest. Also for the match in Hungary, a fans' charter was provided by UK Leisure B.737-400 G-UKLC (UKL9199). Both this aircraft and the Manx Airlines BAe.146 returned in the early hours of the 16th straight after the match, which Manchester United won 3-2. (Nik French)

28th September 1993 - The Honved team arrived today on Malev TU-154 HA-LCH (MAH1680 from Budapest), making its first visit to Manchester before leaving two days later. The game was played the following day, which United won again 2-1 and was looking like they knew how to win games against European opposition. (Denis Norman).

11th October 1993 – Italian airline Fortune made their first visit to Manchester with DC-9-15 I-TIAN, which brought in Ancona for the following evening's game with Bolton Wanderers. The aircraft arrived from Birmingham, having dropped off another Italian side, Pescara, who were due to play West Brom also on the 12th October. The airline made two visits in 1993, but ceased trading the following year, when it re-launched as Norman. Interestingly, for this aircraft's final visit on the 20th October 1995, it was operating a Brussels flight on behalf of Sabena. (Lee Collins)

18ᵗʰ October 1993 – A new Turkish airline to Manchester, TUR, provided two movements today in connection with Manchester United's latest European adventure. The airline was in existence between 1989 and 1994. During this time they operated five Boeing 727-200s, one Boeing 737-200 and two MD-82 aircraft. MD-82 TC-TRU & B.727-200 TC-RUT both made morning visits today, carrying the Galatasaray team, the press and a number of fans. A further passenger charter today was operated by Istanbul Airlines B.737-400 TC-AYA plus executive BAe.125 TC-COS.
(Above Lee Collins, below Nik French)

The highest-placed English and Italian side from each group would go forward to the final, which would be played at Wembley in March 1994. However, their results were not good enough to see them progress into the semi-finals. The tournament would continue for a further season before being dropped altogether. Fixture congestion was the reason given for the termination of the competition. The Anglo-Italian Cup provided one more football charter when Brescia arrived on the 9th November aboard TEA Italy B.737-300 I-TEAA to play a match with Stoke City.

The format of the UEFA Champions League was now in its second year since it had been revised. It was no longer a straightforward two-legged knockout tournament, although the first two rounds remained as such. The successful teams then went to a group stage, before reverting to a knockout phase again for the semi-finals. Manchester United successfully overcame Honved in the first round, but again faltered in the next round, going out on away goals to Galatasaray. But the season wasn't all bad, as they retained the Premier League and also won the FA Cup Final, which ensured they would be in the Champions League again the following season.

2nd November 1993 – After a disappointing 3-3 draw with Galatasaray two weeks earlier, Manchester United had travelled to Turkey today knowing that nothing less than victory would be good enough. The team left aboard Air 2000 B.757 G-OOOI, which was also accompanied by two fans' charters, Caledonian B.757 G-BPEA (CKT7577) and Monarch Airlines A.300 G-MAJS (MON2167) seen here. More disappointment would follow as United only managed a 0-0 draw, which meant they exited Europe again. A number of fans due to return on Caledonian B.757 G-BPEA were detained by Turkish authorities for a 'number of disturbances'. (Paul Rowland)

SEASON 1994/1995
Manchester United UEFA Champions League

The 1994–95 UEFA Champions League was the fortieth year of UEFA's premier European Club football tournament, and the third since its rebranding as the UEFA Champions League. The tournament was won by Ajax of the Netherlands, with a late goal in the final against defending champions Milan of Italy. Ajax won the competition without losing a game, either in the group or the knockout stage in winning the title for the first time since 1973. Compared to the previous year, radical changes were made to the format of the European Cup.

12th September 1994 - SAS Fokker F.28 SE-DGA is seen having just arrived with IFK Gothenburg. This aircraft was formerly operated by Swedish domestic airline, Linjeflyg. Although Linjeflyg was 50% owned by SAS, they were considered too much of a threat to SAS, so in February 1992 they purchased the last 50% in Linjeflyg to perpetuate their dominance. On 1st January 1993, Linjeflyg was merged into SAS, which at the time was the largest Fokker F.28 operator in the world. F.28 SE-DGA departed Manchester in the early hours of the 15th, only to return shortly afterwards with handling problems. It retreated to the FLS hangar for attention, before finally departing on the 17th. The Gothenburg team were dispatched to the departure lounge, and provided with tea and sandwiches before leaving on the early morning SAS flight (SAS1540) operated by MD-80 OY-KHF. (Geoff Ball)

This season included four groups of four teams each in the group stage, an increase from two groups of four teams each in 1993–94. It was also the first year in which eight teams advanced to the knockout stage and the first of three years in which champions of smaller nations entered the UEFA Cup instead of the Champions League. Unfortunately the new format did not improve Manchester United's fortunes. Included in the group were their conquerors from last season, Galatasaray. Even though they did beat them 4-0 at home, they finished third out of the four teams in Group A and were eliminated from the competition. This was also the season when Manchester United battled with Blackburn Rovers to retain their Premier League title. Yet again there was disappointment, when despite Blackburn losing on the last day of the season to Liverpool, United could have nicked the title by winning away to West Ham United, but they only managed a draw meaning Blackburn won the title by a mere one point. The season was rounded off by losing the FA Cup Final to Everton.

Manchester United's next European match was away to Galatasaray on the 28th September, where they managed a 0-0 draw. So after two matches they had four points and things weren't looking too bad. However, the 'wobble' began on the 19th October when Barcelona came to town, which only provided Air Europa B.757 EC-FFK (AEA3555 from Barcelona), which carried the team, their officials and a small number of fans. The game was a disappointing 2-2 draw, but United were still in a good position to go forward to the next round. However, these hopes quickly evaporated when they travelled to Barcelona to play the return match. The team plus those fans that made the trip returned to Spain aboard Air Europa B.757 EC-FEE (AEA3556), which positioned in from Kosice earlier in the day.

14th September 1994 – Sterling European B.727 OY-SBH seen here on short finals, brought IFK Gothenburg fans to Manchester, to see their team beaten 4-2 later that evening. The roots of the airline could be traced back to 1962, when they purchased their first two Douglas DC-6 aircraft from Swissair shortly afterwards, before eventually progressing to SE.210 Caravelles and then Boeing 727s in 1973. Unfortunately, on the 29th October 2008 Sterling declared bankruptcy due to the rising fuel prices in the first half of 2008. Their entire fleet was grounded with immediate effect, thus bringing down the curtain on the airline after forty-six years. (Geoff Ball)

5ᵗʰ December 1994 – Air Alfa B.727-230 TC-ALK (LFA1188 from Istanbul) was the first of two football charters today, both in connection with the Galatasaray and Manchester United match two days later. Launched in 1992, this was the airline's first visit to Manchester. In 1998 they operated a short series of weekly flights from/to Dalaman with A.300 & A.320 aircraft, but would eventually file for bankruptcy in 2002. TC-ALK, the only one of the airline's Boeing 727s to visit Manchester and formerly operated by Lufthansa as D-ABCI, brought in the Galatasaray team and officials. (Ian Hawkridge)

5ᵗʰ December 1994 – The second Turkish football charter today, THY B.727 TC-JCB (THY3101 from Istanbul), bought in more Galatasaray fans. One of the last few remaining Boeing 727s in service with the airline at the time, it was sold in 2000 to Transmile Air Service as 9M-TGA. (Geoff Ball)

4th June 1995 - With the dissolution of the Soviet Union in 1991, Latvia became one of the fifteen independent states which emerged from the breakup. Although what was particularly interesting about the country and its attempts to form a national carrier, was that this did not take place until the 28th August 1995 when Air Baltic was formed in partnership with Scandinavian Airlines. Two years prior to this however, independent airline LatCharter was formed with a single ex-Aeroflot TU-134, YL-LBE. This aircraft is seen here at Manchester having just arrived with the Latvian U-21 football team. It had initially flown from Riga to Belfast, where it dropped off the senior side before flying to Manchester to drop off the 'juniors'. After just under a two hour stay, it departed for Manston where it parked up until the 8th, when it positioned back to Manchester to collect the under-21s before leaving for Belfast. TU-134 YL-LBE operated for LatCharter until 2003, when it was sold as UN-65695. (Lee Collins)

SEASON 1995/1996
Manchester United UEFA Cup
Blackburn Rovers UEFA Champions League
Liverpool UEFA Cup
Wrexham European Cup Winners' Cup
Anglo-Italian Cup (Oldham & Stoke)
Euro '96 Qualifier (Ireland & Netherlands)

The end of last season saw Manchester United narrowly miss out on the silverware from two competitions. They lost the Premier League by one point to Blackburn, in a nail biting final game of the season and were also beaten in the FA Cup Final by Everton. Although it meant they still qualified for Europe, albeit via the UEFA Cup, it was yet another disappointing European campaign as they were knocked in the first round by Russian Cup finalists, Rotor Volgograd, on the away goals rule. However, out of disappointment came triumph this season as they won the Premier League for the second time and the FA Cup by beating Liverpool 1-0.

The first football charter of this particular season, which provided a wide range of football related charters not just from Manchester United, was early in the season and provided by Wrexham. The Welsh side were taking part in European action for the first time since being knocked out of the European Cup by Manchester United in 1990. Their opposition this time came in the form of Romanian team, Petrolul Ploiesti, who arrived on Tarom IL-18 YR-IMG which stayed for three days. This flight had been programmed to arrive at Manchester some weeks in advance, despite the possibility that it might be re-routed through Liverpool instead.

There was also a rumour that a Moldovan Ilyushin IL-18 would turn up with fans, but this never materialised. The home leg ended in a 0–0 draw, but Wrexham lost 1–0 in the away leg, with the Romanians scoring the only goal of the match, and Wrexham being subsequently knocked out of the tournament.

In only their third season in the top flight, Blackburn Rovers won the Premier League the previous season, beating Manchester United to the title by one point. This gave them entrance to the European Champions League for the first time. Drawn into Group B, their opponents would be Spartak Moscow, Legia Warsaw and Rosenborg. Their first match was played on the 13th September 1995. Aeroflot Tupolev TU-154 RA-85648 (AFL2245 from Moscow) had arrived the previous day with Spartak Moscow, who went back to Russia with a 1-0 victory.

12th September 1995 - Manchester United were entered into the UEFA Cup with the first match taking place today against Russian-side Rotor Volgograd, where the first-leg ended 0-0. Air 2000 B.757 G-OOOW (AMM898) provided the transport for United and their officials. The second leg at Old Trafford on the 26th September was a very disappointing 2-2 draw. This meant that Rotor Volograd went through on away goals and the end of United's European hopes for another season.

26th September 1995 - Euralair B.737 F-GJDL (EUL015P) arrived from Leeds to fly AS Monaco out, because of late-night noise restrictions at Leeds.

27th September 1995 - British World BAe.146 G-BTZN (BWL2089) flew the team out to Trondheim to play Rosenborg. Again the result was disappointing, as they were beaten 2-1 by the Norwegian side. For all but the final group matches, the team would use Blackpool as their staging post for flights abroad within the group. Having picked only one point from five matches, Blackburn was already out of the competition. For their final game, which was at home against Rosenborg, their Norwegian opponents arrived at Manchester on the 5th December aboard Braathens B.737-400 LN-BRQ (BRA1279 from Trondheim). Although Blackburn won the match 4-1, the result was academic and B.737 LN-BRQ arrived again on the 7th to collect Rosenborg.

11th - 14th December 1995 - This period produced a large number of charters for a Euro '96 playoff match between Ireland and Holland, to be played at Anfield on the 13th December 1995, when the majority of the flights took place. The Dutch FA decided to send all their official flights to Manchester rather than Liverpool, fearing they would not be able to cope. And not surprisingly when the airport put 4,000 passengers in an hour through security after the match, their decision was entirely justified. All flights operated from T2, with most announcements in Dutch! The runway night closures taking place during this time were suspended for one night only. The Dutch team arrived on the 11th onboard Transavia B.737-300 PH-HVF (TRA7595), and left on the 14th aboard PH-HVV (TRA7561/2). These flights produced numerous interesting aircraft, namely Dutch-registered Sabena Dash-8 PH-SDP which arrived at 1313 (SCH302 from Rotterdam) and returned later in the evening at 2216 to operate SCH305 outbound to Rotterdam.

Martinair also did the same thing with B.767-300 PH-MCL (MPH4663 and MPH4665), their only flights during this period. The main operator was Transavia, with six different B.737-300s during the 12th/13th, PH-HVF, HVG, HVT, HVV & TSX. All of these aircraft operated several flights, along with sole B.757, PH-TKC (14th) which was also a first visit. Since KLM had relinquished their operations at Manchester to Air UK, their visits were non-existent, but today two flights were operated by B.737s PH-BDU (KLM1057) & PH-BDO (KLM1067). Air Holland B.737-300 PH-OZB made two visits, whilst EuroBelgian provided two B.737-400 charters: OO-SBN (EBA1377/8 from/to Brussels) & OO-LTS (EBA1379/80 from/to Amsterdam). British airlines such as Monarch, Britannia and Sabre Airways were also involved, and there were also a number of Irish flights although the majority of these used Liverpool. Ryanair alone provided an extra fifty-four flights during this period. A large number of passengers also used scheduled flights on the proceeding and succeeding days.

8th August 1995 – Tarom Ilyushin IL18 YR-IMG (ROT5393 from Bucharest) is seen resting between its football related duties. The airline had operated IT flights between Manchester and the Black Sea resort of Constanta continuously from 1970-1994. In 1994 they commenced a twice-weekly scheduled service from/to Bucharest lasting until March 1996. Today's visit of YR-IMG was the last to Manchester of a Tarom Ilyushin IL-18, although another Romanian operator, Romavia, sent IL-18 YR-IMZ on two occasions during December 1998. YR-IMG operated for Tarom until 2000 before being sold in April 2001 as ER-ICG. (Geoff Ball)

4th September 1995 - The Anglo-Italian Cup was played for the final time this season, and involved local teams Oldham Athletic and Stoke City. TEA Belgium OO-LTL (EBA1102) flew Oldham to Cagliari today for a group match the following evening with Ancona. Having been defeated 1-0, Oldham returned to Manchester on the 8th aboard SAS MD80 LN-RMF (SK7540). (Nik French)

24th September 1995 – Aeroflot Yakolev YAK-42 RA-42361 (AFL3037 from Moscow) arrived at Manchester today with the Rotor Volgograd team and officials. A further fans' charter flight planned for the 26th was cancelled because the fans couldn't get their UK visas in time. (Lee Collins)

25th September 1995 – Vnukovo Airlines, a new airline to Manchester, provided Tupolev TU-154M RA85621 (VKO2825 from Moscow) as the transport for another Russian team,

Spartak Vladikavkaz. It arrived at Manchester unusually, because Vladikavkaz were due to play Liverpool FC the following evening in a UEFA Cup second round match. It became touch and go whether the flight would arrive at all, as the neccessary documentation had yet to be issued. But the aircraft did arrive, only to be immediately impounded whilst the airline sent on the documents for insurance etc to the Department of Transport. This was only just sorted out prior to its scheduled departure after the match. Making its second visit, having previously visited with Aeroflot, this aircraft was written off less than one year later, when on the 29th August 1996 whilst on a flight from Moscow-Vnukovo Airport, it crashed into mountains on approach to Svalbard-Longyearbyen Airport in Norway, killing all 141 onboard. (Lee Collins)

10th October 1995 – DC-9-15 I-TIAR (NOM576) was the transport for two Italian sides, Cesena and Salernitana, who were to play Oldham and Stoke respectively the following evening. Neither side fared too well in the final Anglo-Italian Cup competition, with both finishing low down in their respective groups. This aircraft, formerly operated by Fortune Aviation, was now being used by another short-lived Italian outfit, Norman. (Lee Collins)

EURO '96

The humble beginnings of the bidding process for Euro '96 went back to 1991. Interested countries were asked to submit their plans to UEFA by the 10th December 1991. At the time, there was uncertainty as to the whether the tournament would be extended to include sixteen teams, so bids were largely based on an eight team tournament. The hosting of the event was contested by five countries: Austria, England, Greece, Netherlands and Portugal. The English bid was selected by UEFA at a meeting on the 5th May 1992. In the year preceding the decision, the English FA had dropped their plans to also bid for the 1998 World Cup in order to gain support of other UEFA members who were to bid for that event.

Matches were to be played during the period 8th – 30th June. There were initially four groups, (A-D) with four teams in each. One team within each group was seeded and played all its matches at the same location. (* - seeded teams/locations).

Group A: England*, Scotland, Netherlands, Switzerland. (Matches played at Wembley and Villa Park).

Group B: Spain*, Bulgaria, France, Romania. (Matches played at Elland Road* and St.James Park).

Group C: Germany*, Czech Republic, Italy, Russia. (Matches played at Old Trafford* and Anfield)

Group D: Denmark*, Croatia, Portugal, Turkey. (Matches played at Hillsborough* and City Ground, Nottingham).

8th June 1996 - The opening match of the tournament took place today between England and Switzerland at Wembley, resulting in a disappointing 1-1 draw.

9th June 1996 -   The games taking place today were Germany-Czech Republic at Old Trafford, Denmark-Portugal at Hillsborough and Spain-Bulgaria at Elland Road. A series of flights by Premiair operated on the 8th/9th using Airbus A.300 OY-CNL to bring in Danish fans from Copenhagen. Other charters for the Denmark v Portugal game were Maersk B.737-500s OY-APA (DMA817) & OY-APB (DMA897), both arriving during the morning and returning after the match. Other charters connected with this fixture were Newair Fokker F.27 OY-MUF (NAW1703) and Citation 550 OY-BZT (BDI588). Translift A.300 EI-TLB (TLA390) & Air Atlanta L.1011 TF-ABH (ABD100) were also involved, both operating inbound charters from Billund. This match also produced the first visit of a Portugalia Fokker Fk-100, CS-TPF, PGA6610 from Oporto). The Czech fans arrived on some interesting charters, in particular a couple of nice Ilyushin IL-62s. The first, ex CSA machine OK-JBJ (PGU310 from Prague), was carrying Bemoair titles, while the other, OK-BYV (PGU310A from Prague) was a Government machine with both using Air Prague flight numbers. Bemoair sprung a surprise, with the unprogrammed appearance and a first visit of type of one of their LET410s, OK-WDO (BMI301 from Prague). While the Germans produced the following flights: Lufthansa B.737-300 D-ABEH (DLH1870 from Frankfurt), first visit Eurowings ATR-42 D-BBBB (EWG2168 from Cologne), Lufthansa A.321 D-AIRD on the morning Frankfurt flight (DLH4068), Gill Air ATR-42 G-ORFH (GIL211M from Frankfurt) plus executive traffic Beech 200 D-IMDA, Citation 550 D-

IMME & Citation 560 D-CTAN. Hemus Air Tupolev TU-134 LZ-TUT which was due into Manchester for the Spain-Bulgaria game on the 8th was cancelled at the last minute.

10th June 1996 - The Danish fans went home on Premiair DC-10 OY-CNU (VKG454) and Premiair Airbus A.300 OY-CNK (VKG464) having seen their team play out a 1-1 draw. Another Gill Air flight took German fans back to Frankfurt, this time operated by ATR-42 G-BVJP (GIL211F) with Lufthansa again producing some equipment upgrades on their Frankfurt flights, A.300 D-AIAT (f/v) & A.321 D-AIRE.

Two of the three games today took place at Birmingham and Newcastle, so nothing arrived at Manchester for these matches, although there were still plenty of interesting charters. While the third match taking place today, Russia-Italy at Anfield, did produce some good Russian visitors, nothing came from Italy. The Gazpromavia Yakovlev Yak-42 RA-42436 made a further visit, but the highlight was the first visit of type by the Ilyushin IL-86 which had eluded Manchester so far, but today there were two examples in connection with this match. They missed out on being on the ground simultaneously by just ninety minutes. Aeroflot IL-86 RA-86054 (AFL249B from Moscow) arriving at 0925 was the first of these mighty machines. Co-incidentally, Aeroflot used Euro '96 to re-introduce their scheduled flights to Moscow, which had been suspended since January 1996 but ceased again, permanently this time in January 1997. The second Ilyushin IL-86 was Transaero RA-86123 at 1701 (TSO3051 from Moscow), marking the airline's second appearance at Manchester, with the first on the 12th April when B.757 EI-CJX arrived for maintenance with British Airways. The match was a disappointment for the Russians, as the Italian side just did enough to produce a victory, winning 2-1.

13th June 1996 - Matches taking place were Bulgaria-Romania at St.James Park and Switzerland-Netherlands at Vila Park, Birmingham, so there were no local charters today.

14th June1996 - Anfield played host to Czech Republic-Italy this evening. This match should have produced a further visit by Ilyushin IL-62 OK-BYU, but its late departure would have broken overnight noise restrictions, so it operated from Liverpool instead! The game between Portugal-Turkey at City Ground, Nottingham was due to produce a number of Air Alfa and Onur Air flights, but this did not happen.

15th June 1996 - The first arrival today was the nocturnal visit of Portugalia Fk-100 CS-TPB (PGA6610/1) collecting Portuguese fans for the match with Turkey. The only match in the North today was the highlight of Group B, France v Spain at Elland Road. The Spanish managed to get most of the limited slots available at Leeds, which was sufficient for their purposes. The French did not, and were forced to operate some charters from Manchester. Air Liberte were early arrivals with both DC-10 F-GPVE at 0822 (LIB8027 from Paris-CDG) & Airbus A.300 F-GHEG at 1040 (LIB8024 from Paris-CDG). French domestic airline Air Inter made their first visits to Manchester with Airbus A.320 F-GHQB at 1105 (ITF9511 from Paris-Orly) & Airbus A.330-300 F-GMDB at 1140 (ITF9502 from Paris-Orly). Air Littoral produced Fokker Fk-100 F-GLIR at 1518 (LIT018 from Marseilles) and Air Atlanta L.1011 TF-ABH (ABD1208 from Beauvais) also operated a fans' charter. In preparation for games the next day, Premiair kept up the shuttle flights with both A.300s OY-CNK & OY-CNL plus Sterling B.727 OY-SBI at 2029 (SNB1331 from Copenhagen) with Danish fans. A number of German charters operating today were

European BAC 1-11 G-AVMY at 1645 (EAF2873 from Frankfurt), EuroBelgian B.737-300 OO-LTP at 1224 (EBA1455 from Frankfurt) and two Lufthansa charters, A.320 D-AIQM at 0748 (DLH 4090 from Frankfurt) & B.737-300 D-ABES at 1146 (DLH4102 from Cologne) as well as the following equipment changes, A.300s D-AIAN (DLH4012) & D-AIAT (DLH4068 and A.321 D-AIRD (DLH4026).

16th June 1996 - With Denmark playing Croatia at Hillsborough, Sheffield and Germany entertaining Russia at Old Trafford, it was hardly surprising that today was going to be busy. Early morning Danish arrivals were Premiair A.300 OY-CNL at 0639 (VKG453 from Copenhagen), another visit by Maersk B.737-500 OY-APA at 0725 (DMA897 from Copenhagen) and Translift A.300 EI-TLB at 0919 (TLA394 from Billund, all of which positioned out. Later in the day saw two Newair F.27s, OY-EBA at 1210 (NAW2758 from Copenhagen) & OY-MUF at 1233 (NAW1704 from Copenhagen); Nordic East L.1011 SE-DPX at 1257 (ELN7757 from Billund) plus North Flying A/S Metroliner OY-NPC at 1110 (NFA171 from Hamburg) & Jetair Metroliner OY-JER at 1211 (FOX061 from Rosklide), all of which day-stopped. After the match, the Maersk B.737 reappeared, as did the Translift A.300 supplemented by Premiair DC-10 OY-CNY at 2301 (VKG8453 from Copenhagen). There were also quite a few day charters with German fans. The first to arrive was Hamburg Air BAe.146 D-AQUA at 0851 (HAS8400 from Cologne). Others during the day were Ratioflug Fokker F.27 D-ADUP at 1022 (RAT027 from Frankfurt), the first visit to Manchester of Augsburg Airways with Dash-8 D-BIRT at 1203 (AUB8086 from Augsburg) and another visit from Eurowings, this time with ATR-42 D-BCRN at 1303 (EWG2180 from Cologne) in full Eurowings colours. Gill Air again operated today with ATR-42 G-ORFH at 1236 (GIL211M from Antwerp). Lufthansa upgraded equipment on one of its scheduled flights (DLH4068) with A.321 D-AIRD and also a charter using B.737-500 D-ABFB (DLH1874 from Frankfurt).

German executive visitors today were Learjet D-CGPD (ATJ161 from Dusseldorf), Citation 550 D-CTAN, Citation 650 D-CLUE and Beech 200s D-IMDA & D-IOAN. Disappointingly, there was no sign of any Russian bizjets, although a BAe.125 had booked a slot for today, which was later cancelled.

17th June 1996 - Premiair A.300 OY-CNL operated an early outbound flight to Copenhagen (VKG456), having arrived at 0319 operating an Airtours flight (AIH190 from Palma) and a further flight (VKG464 to Billund) later the same day. Gill Air ATR-42 G-BVJP (GIL221F) operated outbound to Frankfurt, with Lufthansa operating two A.320s on scheduled flights, D-AIPM (DLH4052) & D-AIQM (DLH4068). Learjet 55 D-CAVE arrived at 1442 (AMB328 f/t Berlin) to collect injured German striker Oliver Bierhoff.

18th June 1996 - With all matches being played today outside of the North West: Scotland-Switzerland at Villa Park, Birmingham, France-Bulgaria at St.James Park, Newcastle and Romania-Spain at Elland Road, Leeds, there were no football charters. However, Lufthansa upgraded equipment with A.300 D-AIAT (DLH4068) and A.320s D-AIQB (DLH4026 & DLH4052) & D-AIPM (DLH5248).

19th June 1996 - This was the busiest day of Euro '96 for Manchester, which would possibly see the biggest match of the tournament so far, the Group C clash between Germany and Italy. Up to this point, the Italian fans seemed to have decided it wasn't worth travelling until their team got into the knockout stage. From a fanatical football nation, there were only a few charters. Alitalia kept the national flag flying with MD-83 I-DAWO at 1548 (AZA8208 from Rome), but this had visited before. More Italian fans arrived, very patriotically on an Air Charter B.737 F-GFLV at 1018 (ACF1770 from Milan) and Centennial MD-83 EC-FZQ at 1425 (CNA435 from Milan). Italian executive visitors were a little more interesting, with Citation 500 I-KWYJ, Benetton operated Citation 650 I-BETV, Learjet 35 I-DLON and Falcon 50 I-CAFD which was met by AS.355 Squirrel G-BUZI to take its passengers to Salford Quays and bring them back immediately after the game.

Many German fans were already here, but more arrived for the day on Crossair MD81 HB-IUH at 0757 (CRX8312) sporting a spectacular 'McDonalds' livery; Lauda Air B.767-300 OE-LAU at 1501 (LDA2087 from Cologne) along with yet another Eurowings ATR-42, D-BFFF at 1359 (EWG2182 from Nuremberg). A second visit was made by North Flying A/S Metroliner OY-NPC at 1744 (NFA131 from Hamburg). British aircraft also played a big role, with European BAC 1-11 G-AVMY at 1220 (EAF2875 from Frankfurt), Gill Air ATR-42 G-BVJP at 1252 (GIL211M from Frankfurt), Titan BAe.146 G-ZAPK at 1826 from Cork and two Air Holland B.757s, G-MONC at 1333 (AHR831) & PH-AHI at 1458 (AHR940), which both arrived from Cologne with the former aircraft on lease from Monarch Airlines. Lufthansa equipment upgrades were A.300 D-AIAR (DLH4058), A.320s D-AIPC (DLH4012) & D-AIQB (DLH4026) and A.321 D-AIRM (DLH4068). There were many other executive visitors arriving for this match, starting with the Germans in the order they arrived: Falcon 20 D-CBNA at 1008, Beech 200 D-IVHM at 1108 & 1651, Citation 560 D-CZAR at 1140, Cessna 421 D-IDIR at 1436, Citation 560 at 1449, P.68 Victor D-GEMA at 1510, Beech 200 D-ILIN at 1632, Learjet 55 D-CREW at 1704, Beech 200 D-IAHK at 1841 and Beech 200 D-IANA at 2015. The highlight was possibly the first visit of German Air Force CL-601 Challenger 12+01 at 1809 from Cologne.

British interest in the match was supplied by BAe.125 G-OMGG (MGC635), Citation 550 G-JCFR (CFR333) & Learjet G-GJET (GMA464). As if this match wasn't creating enough extra traffic, the Turkey-Demark match being played today at Hillsborough brought in Danish fans in large numbers. Once again Premiair used A.300 OY-CNL at 1101 (VKG455 from Copenhagen) & DC-10 SE-DHS at 1200 (VKG453 from Billund), which both returned after the match. Sabre Airways who obviously had enough slack in their summer programme, used two Boeing 727s on flights from Copenhagen: G-BPND at 123 (SBE9204) & G-BNNI at 1148 (SBE9202). Finally there were two Danish Metroliners: OY-JEO at 1006 (FOX062 from Rosklide) & OY-JER at 1550 (FOX006 from Rotterdam) and another extremely late visit by Newair Fokker F.27 OY-EBA at 1909 (NAW9758 from Billund). Two other matches being played today, Russia-Czech Republic at Anfield and Croatia-Portugal did not produce any additional visitors. This final round of games saw the end of the group stages. From our group, Germany won to stay in the north with the Czechs runners up. In Group B was France and Spain, Group D Portugal and Croatia and finally England and Netherlands were in Group A, meaning Denmark, who had been a source of good numbers were eliminated.

20th June 1996 - Having seen their team exit the competition the previous evening, the exodus of foreign fans returning home began today in earnest. Russian fans departed on Gazpromavia Yak 42 RA-42436 (GZP9046 to Vnukovo) and on the second visit of Transaero Ilyushin IL-86 RA-86123 (TSO3052 to Moscow-SVO). Aeroflot however produced another different IL-86, RA-86096 (AFL250B to Moscow-SVO). To date these three IL-86s visiting during Euro '96 have been the only ones to Manchester.

Danish fans departed aboard Premiair A.300 OY-CNL (VKG452 to Billund) & Sterling European B.727 OY-SEZ (SNB1332 to Copenhagen). Even though there were no Swiss fans based in the North West, two charters taking fans back to Zurich were TEA Switzerland B.737-300 HB-IIF (TSW7407) & Crossair MD80 HB-IUF (CRX8419). Although Germany was through to the quarter-finals, there were obviously many fans that had to return home. Lufthansa operated A.321 D-AIRF (FLH4231 to Frankfurt) and B.737-500 D-ABJD (DLH4053 to Dusseldorf), as well as upgrading the equipment on some of their scheduled flights: A.300s D-AIAS (DLH4012) & D-AIAU (DLH4068) and A.321 D-AIRC (DLH4026 & DLH4052). German charter flights as follows were all outbound to Frankfurt: Sabre Airways B.727 G-BPND (SBE9197), Air Jet BAe.146 F-GOMA (AIJ2416), Gill Air ATR-42 G-ORFH (GIL211F) and Ratioflug Fokker F.27 D-ADUP (RAT027). Rather difficult to explain was the re-appearance of Bemoair Let-410 OK-WDO at 1649 (BMI301 from Prague), bearing in mind the next match for the Czech Republic was in Birmingham! Perhaps they had hoped their team would win the group and stay at Old Trafford! In any event it stayed until the 24th, the day after the match. Two teams also passed through, the first was the Italian team trying to escape from their bus into the terminal whilst being perused by the world's media. They were transported home aboard Alitalia MD80 I-DAWU (AZA8211 to Rome-FCO) which was a first visit.

The French team arrived at Manchester from their group base at Newcastle on British World BAC 1-11 G-OBWE at 1456 (BWL7366). Their next match was going to be at Anfield on 22nd, but they insisted on flying down from their base at Newcastle and using a British World 1-11 for the purpose!

21st June 1996 - The only football flight was the return home of the Russian team, when Yakolev Yak-42 turned up again, RA-42436 (GZP9044), departing back to Vnukovo.

22nd June1996 - The first pair of quarter-finals were held today, England v Spain at Wembley and France v Holland at Anfield. It should be remembered that the trips for this phase of the competition had to be arranged very quickly, and as a consequence numbers weren't necessarily as high as fans may not have been able to get the time off work etc. After their successful use of Manchester in the playoff against Ireland at Anfield last December, the Dutch flights used Manchester. Three Transavia aircraft appeared: B.737-300s PH-HVF at 0817 (TRA7503) & PH-HVI at 1004 (TRA7505) and B.757 PH-TKB at 1038 (TRA7501), which all left after dropping off their passengers. After the match another three positioned in for the return flights: B.737-300s PH-HVJ (TRA7526) & PH-TSZ (TRA7504) and B.757 PH-TKA (TRA7502). Also making appearances were Translift A.300 EI-CJK at 0923 (TLA460), Nordic East L.1011 SE-DPX at 0929 (ELN7755), Martinair B.767-300 PH-MCI at 1027 (MPH4769) and passenger-configured Emerald Airways BAe.748 G-BVOV at 1054 (JEM1057). In the evening Air

Holland B.757 PH-AHE (AHD994) arrived at 2343 to collect returning fans. Private visitors today were well represented with two Martinair Citation 650s: PH-MEX at 1312 (MPH4509) & PH-MFX at 1344 (MPH4511), Citation 550 OY-CYT at 1340 (ALS5079), Beech 200 D-ICSM at 1232, Cessna 210 N9210Y at 1348 & PA-31 Navajo N528WA at 1348. The latter two arrived from Rotterdam with Dutch pilots! Virtually all the French traffic went into Liverpool, with the exception of Air Inter A.300 F-BUAI at 1445 (IFT9512 from Paris-Orly). Finally, ahead of tomorrow's match between Germany and Croatia at Old Trafford, Citation 550 S5-BAC arrived at 1615 from Zagreb with a number of Croatian dignitaries, including the Croatian president, Mr. Franjo Tudman. It departed the following evening after the match.

23rd June 1996 - Today's quarter-finals involved the Czech Republic-Portugal, being played at Villa Park and Germany-Croatia at Old Trafford. If only the German opponents were Denmark and not Croatia! Based on the way their fans had supported their national side up to this point, today could have been a bumper day for the airport and its enthusiasts. However, the Croatians provided no additional charters and the only two executive visitors were Falcon 10 9A-CRL at 0949 & Citation 501 HB-VLB at 1109, both from Zagreb. German executive visitors fared a little better with Beech 200s D-ICRA, D-IOAN & D-IUUU, Cessna 340 D-IAGC, Cessna 337 D-ICWS, Cessna 421 D-ITAS, Citation 550 D-CHDE and Citation 650 D-CLUE. German charters were confined to Aero Lloyd MD83, D-ALLN at 1200 (AEF076 from Dusseldorf), Gill Air ATR-42 G-ORFH at 0952 (GIL211M from Frankfurt) & North Flying A/S Metroliner OY-NPC at 1124 (NFA171 from Hamburg). Lufthansa provided B.737-300 D-ABJH at 0924 (DLH1874 from Cologne) and Airbus A.310 D-AIDC (DLH4068). Also in connection with today's game was the visit from/to Halton of Cessna 177 G-AZFP. The tournament was over for the Dutch. Having been beaten by France, the team left from Manchester aboard Transavia B.737-300 PH-TSX (TRA7804). The final outcome of today's game was that Germany beat Croatia 2-1 and after monumental struggle at Villa Park, the Czech Republic beat Portugal 1-0.

24th June 1996 - The vanquished Portuguese team, beaten by the Czech Republic, must have been staying nearer to Manchester than Birmingham, as they escaped home to Lisbon on Air Portugal B.737-300 CS-TIG (TAP9900).

26th June 1996 - Today would see the final match of Euro '96, to be played at Old Trafford, the first semi-final game between France and the Czech Republic with a 1700 kick off. The other semi-final would be England-Germany at Wembley during the evening. The final of course, would also take place at Wembley four days later. The first football movement today, under very low cloud and drizzle, was Brit Air ATR-42 F-GGLR at 0914 (BZH2751 from Paris-CDG) in full Air France colours. Other French charters during the day were Air Inter A.300 F-BUAI at 1316 (ITF9502 from Par-is-Orly) making its second visit, EuroBelgian B.737-300 OO-LTJ at 1040 (EBA6332 from Paris-CDG), Flanders Air Beech 1990 at 1309 (FRS1999 from Lille) and Regional Airlines Jetstream F-GMVK at 1427 (RGI1602 from Le Bourget). Adding to yesterday's arrival of Falcon 20 F-GLNL, other light visitors for the match were Beech 200 F-GPRB at 1036 (from Le Havre), PA-31 Navajo F-GDRJ at 1209 (from Lille), PA-31 Navajo PH-DAE at 1240 (TLP6A from Reims),

Mooney F-GHMG at 1302 (from Reims), PA-28RT Cherokee F-GLGL at 1339 (from Reims) and Beech 90 F-GHBB at 1456 (from Le Bourget). The Czechs again brought the two mighty Il-62s, OK-JBJ at 1025 (BMI401) & OK-BYV at 1147 (PGU310) and three CSA charters, Tupolev TU-134 OK-HFM at 1009 (CSA7516), Tupolev TU-154 OK-UCE at 1114 (CSA7518) and Czech Govt TU-154 OK-VCP at 1136 (CSA7514). Unfortunately, a further CSA TU-134 and TU-154 flight were both cancelled. The latter aircraft had been booked to arrive for their match on the 9th June, but was later cancelled. Danish Air Transport Beech 1900 OY-JRP at 1216 (DTR4231 from Amsterdam) apparently arrived with a party of Dutch fans on a pre-booked charter, who were assuming their country would be in the semi-finals! Wrong!

And so to the final movements for us. The French were beaten by the Czechs and left on 27th on another Air Inter first visit aircraft, A.320 FGHQC (ITF9501 to Paris-Orly. A couple of other Euro '96 flights were an excursion for the final weekend to Bournemouth, operated by Gill ATR-42 BVJP on the 28th (GIL201M), returning two days on ATR-42 G-ORFH (GIL201M). For those still keeping up with this footballing chapter, the final was played out between Germany and Czech Republic, which was predictably won in extra-time by Germany 2-1. The conclusion of this three week football fest was Manchester recorded around 420 extra movements (including General Aviation traffic), carrying approximately 25,000 fans from ten of the fourteen participating countries.

4th June 1996 –The first team arriving locally for the tournament today were the Danish on SAS MD80 LN-RMA (SAS539 f/Copenhagen). Later today, the Russians arrived in Gazpromavia YAK-42 RA42436 (GZP9043 from Vnukovo). The remainder of the Group C teams arrived in the next couple of days. The Czechs arrived aboard CSA Tupolev TU-134 OK-HFM (CSA7504 from Prague) followed by the Italians who arrived in Alitalia A.321 I-BIXG (AZA8206 from Rome), the first of their new fleet to appear. (Nik French)

5th June 1996 – The last of the 'local' teams to arrive were the Germans at 0913 in the morning sunshine aboard Lufthansa A.321 D-AIRR (DLH1870 f/Frankfurt), which was also a first visit. As far as the fans were concerned, there was a wide range of packages on offer, ranging from day trips to stays of a week or more. Sometimes supporters had to stay considerable distances away from the grounds where the team were playing due to the lack of hotel accommodation. Some of the local teams often had countryside retreats, with the Russians being accommodated in Wigan! (Paul Rowland)

8th June 1996 – Many of Lufthansa's scheduled flights from Manchester during this period had equipment upgrades, such as today's visit of Airbus A.310 D-AIDD (DLH4068 from Frankfurt) on the airline's mid-morning flight. Note the aircraft is carrying 'Express' titles but appears to be in a shabby condition. (Nik French)

9th June 1996 – Premiair A.300 OY-CNL was a regular during Euro '96, ferrying fans between Billund-Copenhagen. It was also regularly used in the summer by Airtours for sub-charters. After a gap of four years, it made its last visit on 4th May 2001 operating another sub-charter for Airtours (AIH217 to Heraklion). Although sold in December 2001 to Bosphorus European as TC-COA, it never flew with this Turkish airline. (Rick Ward)

9th June 1996 – This fine 1988-built machine was delivered to the Czech Government the same year. Leased to Air Georgia and then Air Prague for several years before being withdrawn in 1997, it did not fly for several years. It currently operates as a pure freighter aircraft for KAPO SP Gorbunova, registered as RA-86945. (Paul Rowland)

9th June 1996 – Bemoair Ilyushin IL-62 OK-JBJ was built and delivered to CSA in late 1979, and operated for them until May 1996, when it was sold to Bemoair. In June 1991 it was leased to Malev as HA-LIA in full colours, to operate on their new Budapest-Tokyo route, but it only flew three round-trips before returning to CSA. (Stuart Prince)

9th June 1996 – A fine shot of both Ilyushin IL-62s on the western apron. This was the only occasion when two IL-62s were parked together at Manchester. (Michael Oldham)

9th June 1996 – Eurowings ATR-42 D-BBBB (EWG2168 f/Cologne) still shows signs of a former life. The airline was formed in 1993 with the amalgamation of NFD (Nurnberger Flugdienst) and RFD (Reise-und Industrieflug), inheriting a fleet of ATR-42 & ATR-72 aircraft. This was the airline's first visit to Ringway, although NFD did operate a short-lived scheduled service between April 1987 and March 1988. (Michael Oldham)

9th June 1996 – One of two Maersk B.737-500s making first visits this morning is OY-APA. Having been delivered new earlier in April 1996, it only spent two years with the airline. In 1998 it was leased to Estonian Air until 2000, when it was leased to Tarom for a further year before finally being sold to All Nippon in 2001. This aircraft would make four visits during Euro '96 and its final visit on the 31st July 1998 operating a charter from Hanover. (Denis Norman)

9th June 1996 – Newair Fokker F.27 OY-MUF (NAW1703 from Billund) seen here on short finals, was no stranger to Manchester as it regularly operated Newair twice-weekday service between Manchester and Billund. It made its final visit on the 27th July 1997, just before the airline collapsed later that year. (Denis Norman)

9th June 1996 – Irish operators Translift were frequent visitors to Manchester, initially operating sub-charters for airlines such as Airtours, Britannia Airways and Monarch. They

also had their own programme of flights from 1997. Airbus A.300 EI-TLB is seen here, having recently arrived from Billund on a Euro '96 charter. The airline operated six Airbus A.300s and ceased trading in October 2000. This particular aircraft was withdrawn in October 1999 and broken up the following May. (Nik French)

9th June 1996 – Seen under increasingly cloudy skies, Portugalia Fokker FK-100 CS-TPF (PGA6610 from Oporto) was another airline making its first visit to Manchester. On the 19th May 1997, the airline launched direct services between Manchester and Lisbon for the first time since Air Portugal withdrew from the route in March 1994. Portugalia themselves operated the route, also serving Oporto, until January 2006, using Fokker 100s and also Embraer EMB-145s. (Michael Oldham)

10th June 1996 – Not a million miles away from the Air France livery, Transaero IL-86 RA-86123 seen on very short finals, is perfectly captured with the Airport Hotel providing a suitable backdrop. Delivered to Transaero in July 1992, it operated for them until 2000 when it was leased to Kras Air, Vaso and later Atlant Soyuz until 2010, when the latter airline ceased operations. It was believed to have been broken up by April 2011. (Above Mark White, below Paul Rowland)

10th June 1996 – Ilyushin IL-86 RA-86054 (AFL249B from Moscow) was a first visit of type, with another Aeroflot example, RA-86096, turning up ten days later. RA-86054 was already thirteen years old when it visited Manchester, delivered to Aeroflot as CCCP-86054 on 14th April 1983. It was possibly withdrawn from service around 2004/2005 and reportedly broken up around 2006. (Above Nik French, below Denis Norman)

12th June 1996 – Right in the middle of the Euro '96 fortnight was this outstanding visitor, although nothing to do with the tournament itself! Japanese Air Force B.747-400 20-1101 arrived at 1305 (JAF.1101 from Lyon) on a training flight 'inspecting' Manchester's facilities. The visit was in connection with a G7 summit to be held in Lyon, France later in the year and having landed at Manchester, a crew change was affected and the aircraft left for Gatwick, where a similar operation would take place, just over thirty minutes later. The Japanese consider it unlucky if one of their aircraft carrying Royals or dignitaries has not visited before. (Above Paul Rowland, below Lee Collins)

15ᵗʰ June 1996 – Air Liberte operated five Douglas DC-10s, with today's visit of F-GPVE being the first to Manchester. Its tenure with the French airline was short-lived, as it was sold to Continental Airlines as N37077 in September 1996, operating for five years before being withdrawn at Mojave, California in September 2001. (Michael Oldham)

15ᵗʰ June 1996 – Air Liberte A.300 F-GHEG was also making its only visit to Manchester. One of two aircraft delivered to Air Liberte in early 1990, it was sold in July 1998 to China Airlines. Although Air Liberte folded in 2001, this aircraft is still alive and well, and thirteen years later is operating for FedEx as N740FD. (Nik French)

15th June 1996 – Being predominantly a domestic airline, it was unlikely that Air Inter would ever visit Manchester, but Euro '96 would produce five different aircraft visits. A.320 F-GHQB was the first of two Airbus A.320s making their first visits, with the other being F-GHQC on the 27th June 1996. (Nik French)

15th June 1996 – Air Inter A.330-300 F-GMDB was only the fourth Airbus A.330 to visit Manchester. The previous three had all been Aer Lingus examples during 1994/95. In 2015, this aircraft now operates for Brussels Airlines as OO-SFN. (Michael Oldham)

15th June 1996 – Air Atlanta aircraft were a familiar sight at Manchester throughout the mid to late 1990s. Operating L.1011 Tristars and Boeing 747s, it was not unusual to see anything up to five aircraft parked up in a wide range of liveries, awaiting their next turn of duty. This aircraft, TF-ABH, which was leased to Peach Air during 1997/8 in full colours, made its final visit to Ringway on 13th March 1999 operating KGC4326 to Malaga. It was withdrawn from service later in the month and scrapped at Manston later that year. (Denis Norman)

15th June 1996 – Eurobelgian was set up by November 1991 and began operations during April 1997, based at Brussels. They would eventually operate sixteen different B.737s, a mix of -300 & -400 series. B.737-33A OO-LTP seen here on a football charter from Frankfurt, was bought by the Virgin Group in April 1996 and rebranded Virgin Express. (Lee Collins)

15ᵗʰ June 1996 – With nineteen aircraft and more than 1,300 staff, Sterling celebrated its 25ᵗʰ anniversary in 1987, but by 1993 the airline went bankrupt. The following year it was reborn again as Sterling European, with three aircraft and 182 staff. One of these, OY-SBI, has just arrived on a football charter from Copenhagen. Delivered new to US Air in April 1983, it was the final passenger Boeing 727 built and it operated for Sterling European between 1994 and 1997. Its final operator was US cargo airline, Champion Air, but it was withdrawn in 2008. (Barry Swann)

19ᵗʰ June 1996 – SE-DHS was the second of two Premiair Douglas DC-10s used during the Euro '96 airlift. As part of changes to the Airtours group, of which Premiair was a part, both Airtours and Premiair were rebranded as MyTravel. Their five DC-10s operated the airlines longer routes to holiday areas such as Africa, the Far East and the USA, but they also served Mediterranean destinations to supplement the A.300s. All five DC-10s were transferred to My Travel in 2002. (Geoff Ball)

43

19th June 1996 – Crossair MD80 HB-IUH was making its first visit to Manchester in this fine colour scheme, although it had been in previously operating for Swissair in full Crossair colours. This colourful livery was worn in co-operation with Hotelplan, a Swiss tour operator and McDonald's. It was worn on this aircraft from March 1996 until its removal during April 2000. (Above Mark White, below Geoff Ball)

19th June 1996 – Originally formed in 1969 as Air Charter International, they became simply Air Charter in 1984. B.737-200 F-GFLV seen here operated for two years between 1996 and 1998, prior to the folding of the airline. (Nik French)

19th June 1996 – Sabre Airways began operations in December 1994 with two Boeing 737-200s, G-SBEA & G-SBEB. Two B.727s soon to follow were G-BNNI seen here and G-BPND. Both were regular visitors from 1995-1999, before eventually being replaced by B.737-800s. When a majority share hold was purchased by the Libra Holidays group in November 2000, the name was changed to Excel Airways. (Denis Norman)

19th June 1996 – Yet another operator regularly seen at Manchester, but now consigned to the history books, is Spanish airline Centennial. They began in 1993, operating a weekly summer charter the same year and regular year-round charters until December 1995 when they began a twice-weekly scheduled flight from Manchester to Palma, although in 1996 there was much less emphasis on charter flights. The scheduled service to Palma lasted until November 1996, when the airline ceased trading. (Denis Norman)

19th June 1996 – Today ATR-42 D-BFFF became the third Eurowings aircraft to visit Manchester. Delivered new to NFD in 1989, which later became Eurowings, the aircraft operated until its withdrawal in December 1999, returning to Aerospatiale. (Nik French)

19th June 1996 – Helping to facilitate the movement of German fans, Lauda Air Boeing 767-300 OE-LAU was pressed into service today. The weather so far had been generally pleasant but today was quite cool and cloudy with a moderate easterly wind. Officially merged into Austrian Airlines in July 2012, five Boeing 767-300s are still operated on their long-haul routes, although OE-LAU is not amongst them. It was later sold to XL Airways as G-VKNG in 2004. (Lee Collins)

19th June 1996 – Maybe the fans knew something that the team didn't, as there were few Italian football charters during Euro '96. Today saw the match that Italy had to win if they stood any chance of progressing, but unfortunately they were up against Germany, the eventual winners and the match ended as 0-0 draw. Alitalia MD80 I-DAWO was one of a few charters during the day, bringing fans in from Rome. (Nik French)

19th June 1996 – Jetair Metroliner OY-JEO was another aircraft operating an evening mail/freight flight to Brussels on behalf of Air Bridge Carriers between January and March 1991. It made its first visit to Manchester on the 4th January 1991, and in May 1997 it was sold to Spanish operator, Zorex, as EC-HJC and operated until November 2011 when they lost their Air Operators Certificate. (Denis Norman)

19th June 1996 – German Air Force CL601 Challenger 12+01 arrived with German chancellor Helmut Kohl for this evening's match with Italy. This was the first of only two German military Challengers to visit Manchester; the other was 12+07 on 25th April 1998. Both were sold to civilian operators in 2000 and 2011 respectively. (Geoff Ball)

19ᵗʰ June 1996 – Northern Executive Aviation were kept extremely busy during Euro '96, handling virtually all the executive traffic. Gama Aviation Learjet 35 G-GJET was a regular visitor between 1995 and 2000. In 2001 it was sold as D-CFAI, operating for the United Nations, but it was written off when it aborted takeoff at Kisangani, DR Congo on the 12ᵗʰ June 2008. (Geoff Ball)

19ᵗʰ June 1996 – Learjet 55 D-CREW brought in ex-Wimbledon champion Boris Becker and his party. Operated by MTM Aviation between 1992 and 1997, this was the aircraft's only visit to Manchester. (Geoff Ball)

19ᵗʰ June 1996 – Citation 560 D-CZAR which night-stopped from Munich, was registered to Russian coach Viktor Bondarenko, but it is unknown whether he was onboard. In March 2000 it was traded in for a newer Learjet 45, but registered as VP-CVL. (Geoff Ball)

19ᵗʰ June 1996 – Magec Aviation BAe.125-800 G-OMGG was operated from 2001 to 2004, when it was sold to Gama Aviation and re-registered as G-JJSI. (Geoff Ball)

16th June 1996 – Although going through several identities over the past twenty-five years, the original Hamburg Airlines was founded in April 1988. They operated a single Dornier Do.228 aircraft, but by 1993 after losing money they ceased trading for a short period, but were resurrected in early 1994. They went on to operate three BAe.146 aircraft, the first of which to visit Manchester, D-AQUA, is seen above. However, they experienced financial problems again, and when no buyer or merger partner could be found, they were liquidated in December 1997. (Michael Oldham)

16th June 1996 – Citation 650 D-CLUE was one of several German executive visitors today, arriving for their match with Russia at Old Trafford. This aircraft first visited Manchester on 23rd June 1994, and is still current on the German register twenty-five years after it was first delivered. (Denis Norman)

16th June 1996 – One of two Danish Metroliners today, was North Flying A/S OY-NPC on its first visit to Manchester. Purchased by North Flying A/S in 1995, this Metro made four appearances between 1996 and 2000, and made its last visit on 27th May 2000. It is currently flying in South Africa as ZS-OLS. (Michael Oldham)

16th June 1996 – Another first time visitor today of both the airline and the aircraft was Augsburg Airways Dash-8 D-BIRT. Formed as Intertot Airways and as Augsburg Airways in 1980, they expanded enough to cover various points within Germany. In 1994, they launched International services, including London and Birmingham, but by 2000 they had been absorbed into Team Lufthansa. (Denis Norman)

16th June 1996 – Newair Fokker F.27 OY-EBA, like OY-MUF, would also be used occasionally on the airlines service between Manchester and Billund, but this was far less common. Although the airline folded in September 1997, its last visit to Manchester was actually the 19th June 1996, operating another football charter. (Denis Norman)

16th June 1996 – Jetair Metroliner OY-JER seen here, made its first visit to Manchester on the 25th January 1991. It was one of several Jetair Metros that operated an evening mail/freight flight to Brussels on behalf of Air Bridge Carriers between January and March 1991. In July 1997, it was sold to Spanish operator Zorex as EC-GPE and made five visits between 2006 and 2008. It was withdrawn during 2009 and scrapped at Saragossa soon afterwards. (Denis Norman)

16th June 1996 – Today was the first of two visits by Ratioflug F.27 D-ADUP during Euro '96. Note the starboard wing area is coned off. It made one further visit on 21st October 1997 operating a round trip from Rotterdam, but in December 1997 they ceased trading and the aircraft was parked up at Linz. It is currently stored at Woensdrecht, having recently returned to Fokker after a lease period with PIA. (Michael Oldham)

20th June 1996 – French operator Air Jet had three BAe.146s in service from 1994 to 2002. The aircraft seen here, F-GOMA, had a slightly different livery from the other two, lacking a large blue winged horse on the tail and devoid of any cheatline colours. The airline ceased trading in December 2001. After a period with TNT Airways as a freighter, it is currently operating for the Royal Air Force as ZE707. (Nik French)

20ᵗʰ June 1996 – B.737-300 HB-IIF was the third and final TEA Switzerland aircraft to visit Manchester. The Swiss subsidiary of Trans European Airways survived the collapse of TEA in 1991, but it was purchased by the EasyJet group in 1998, now trading as EasyJet Switzerland. (Geoff Ball)

20ᵗʰ June 1996 – The day was graced by two further Ilyushin IL-86 visits, which would be the last at Manchester. Aeroflot example RA-86096 was a first visit. Delivered new in 1988, it's believed it was withdrawn during 2004 and scrapped around 2007. (Lee Collins)

20th June 1996 – Although this aircraft is featured earlier in the book, for completeness here is another shot of today's visit of Transaero IL-86 RA-86123, seen taxiing for departure. (Geoff Ball)

20th June 1996 – One of the more interesting football charters during Euro '96 is Bemoair Let-410 OK-WDO, seen feet away from touchdown. One of only four different Let-410s to visit Manchester, it came to grief on the 30th October 2005 when it crashed on takeoff at Bergamo on a cargo flight. (Lee Collins)

20th June 1996 – Boeing B.727 OY-SEZ was the tenth and penultimate aircraft from 'Sterling' to visit Manchester, with the final one being OY-SBO on 11th May 1997. OY-SEZ operated until 1999, when it was sold to Sun Country as N294SC, but it never flew with them. (Nik French)

22nd June 1996 – Still going strong after thirty-eight years! Dutch operator Martinair sent B.767-300 PH-MCI to Manchester, with the latest set of football fanatics from Amsterdam. In 1996 the airline still operated a mix of passenger and freight aircraft, but in 2015 they are purely confined to cargo operations. (Denis Norman)

22nd June 1996 – Transavia were another Dutch operator that had been around for a while, first setting up in 1965. Operating aircraft such as the Douglas DC-6, SE.210 Caravelle and the Boeing 707, they were now firmly established as Boeing 737 operators. One such example today was B.737-300 PH-HVF, seen here about to position back to Amsterdam. (Denis Norman)

22nd June 1996 – B.737-300 PH-HVI was the only aircraft amongst today's Transavia contingent making its first visit to Manchester. In 1998, they began to take deliveries of new Boeing 737-800 aircraft, the first of which to make its debut to Ringway was PH-HZF on 26th June 1999. (Denis Norman)

22nd June 1996 – The third Transavia B.737-300 to visit this morning was PH-TSX. Although only twelve months old, it would see less than five years service with the Dutch airline due to the introduction of their new B.737-800s. PH-TSX was withdrawn in November 2000 and sold to Air New Zealand as ZK-NGK. In November 2013 it was withdrawn again and has since been broken up. (Denis Norman)

22nd June 1996 – Transavia also operated three B.757-2K2s from 1993-2003. PH-TKB was the first of two used for today's Netherlands-France match, which proved to be the case of the immovable force against the impenetrable object! Goalless after 90 minutes and extra time, the French eventually became the victors on penalties. (Denis Norman)

22nd June 1996 – Formerly trading as Janes Aviation, they became Emerald Airways in September 1993. The name was reflecting their focus on Irish Sea operations. By the end of 1994 the airline was operating ten BAe.748s. In May 1995 an eleventh aircraft, G-BVOV seen here, was added. As well as cargo and mail operations, they also operated scheduled passenger services between Ronaldsway and Liverpool. Sadly, Emerald Airways is yet another airline that has now disappeared from the scene, after having its AOC revoked on the 5th May 2006. (Denis Norman)

22nd June 1996 – Translift's fleet of Airbus A.300s were frequently leased out to other operators, as well as operating sub-charters. A.300 EI-CJK is seen here having recently arrived from Amsterdam, preparing for its impending fifteen-month lease to Sobelair. On the 10th October 1999 it arrived from Glasgow for attention with FLS, before leaving five days later for storage at Bristol-Filton. (Nik French)

22nd June 1996 – L.1011 SE-DPX started life with TWA as N31024 as a domestic aircraft until 1993, when it was sold to Hawaiian Air who operated it for just under twelve months. In April 1994 it was purchased by Swedish outfit Air Ops. When they ceased trading in May 1996, it was bought by Nordic East, who in turn operated the aircraft until 1997, or their own operations rather than an aircraft available for sub-charters. It was withdrawn at the end of year and scrapped during 1998. (Geoff Ball)

22nd June 1996 – Looking rather shabby above is A.300 F-BUAI, the third different Air Inter aircraft to visit during Euro '96. This was its first visit to Manchester, and it would make its second visit four days later. (Nik French)

23rd June 1996 – Following on from the arrival the previous evening of Citation 550 S5-BAC, Falcon 10 9A-CRL appeared at 0949 from Zagreb with more Croatian dignitaries. This was the aircraft's only visit to Manchester. (Geoff Ball)

23rd June 1996 – D-ALLN was the sixth of ten different Aero Lloyd MD-80s to visit Manchester from 1991 to 1999. By the time of the last visit, made by D-ALLV on 6th May 1999, the airline had begun re-equipping with Airbus A.320 & A.321 aircraft. Since its sale in 1998, it has been operated by Crossair, Swiss Airlines, Viking Airlines and Sky Wings. From September 2010 it's been operated by Khors Air as UR-CJE. (Geoff Ball)

23rd June 1996 – The majority of light and executive aircraft visitors were parked and handled on the South Side. One such example was Citation 650 D-CLUE seen above. In a way it was a 'final hurrah' for the South Side and hangars, as two years later these hangars built in the 1940s were swept away in preparation for Runway 2. (Geoff Ball)

26th June 1996 – The only Brit Air ATR-42 visit was F-GGLR, which day-stopped until the France-Czech Republic game had been played. Set up in 1973 and based at Morlaix, Brittany, the airline started operations two years later, and in 1979 they established a direct link between Brittany and London-Gatwick. On 1st December 1995 Brit Air signed a franchise agreement with Air France and in October 2000 they became a wholly owned subsidiary. The airline had sold its fleet of ATR-42 aircraft by 2005. (Nik French)

26th June 1996 – Making its second visit to Manchester, and the penultimate visit by the French airline, was A.300 F-BUAI. It day-stopped, before departing at 2056 back to Paris-Orly with disappointed French fans, having seen their side knocked out of Euro '96 on penalties. The airline followed a similar fate to that of Brit Air, by being fully integrated into Air France in the late 1990s. (Geoff Ball)

26th June 1996 – Although operating under a EuroBelgian call-sign, B.737-300 OO-LTJ was operating for Air Provence; note the titles, having been leased since January 1996. It returned to full EuroBelgian ownership in November 1996, but was immediately sold on to Frontier Airlines. After a period operating for Garuda Indonesia, it was withdrawn in 2013 and now resides at Goodyear, Arizona. (Nik French)

26ᵗʰ June 1996 – What is evident in both shots of Ilyushin IL-62s OK-JBJ & OK-BYV is that this unique aircraft features not only a manually-operated rudder, but manually operated elevators in the tailplane, which could be hydraulically adjusted for flight trimming. The position of the tail rudder seen here, in a typical position on landing, had corrected itself to the level position once on stand. (Both photos Geoff Ball)

26th June 1996 – CSA would occasionally use Russian aircraft on their Prague schedules from Manchester. In fact, during the winter of 1993/94, one of the three-weekly services was operated by a TU-134. TU-154 substitutions would also occasionally happen. OK-UCE was newly delivered to CSA in June 1989, and served with them until January 2000. (Nik French)

26th June 1996 – This is the second and final visit of TU-154 OK-VCP. The first was on the 2nd September 1993 operating CSA's Prague service. In October 1999 it was sold to Omsk Avia as RA-85841, but it ended its days flying for Atlant-Soyuz Airlines, before they went into liquidation in January 2011. It has since been scrapped. (Geoff Ball).

26th June 1996 – Beech 1900 OY-JRP was the first Danish Air Transport aircraft to visit Manchester, but not today, it was actually 20th June 1995. The airline was set up in 1989, initially as a cargo airline. Soon operating specialist flights such as live horse transportation and delivering supplies for the Paris-Dakar rally. Passenger charter flights began in 1994, with the subsequent launch of scheduled services in November 1996. Five Beech 1900s were operated between 1994 and 2008. This aircraft, OY-JRP, was sold in October 1996 as N505RH. (Geoff Ball)

26th June 1996 – A mid-afternoon line-up consists of Czech Govt TU-154 OK-VCP, EBA/Air Provence B.737-300 OO-LTJ, CSA TU-134 OK-HFM & TU-154 OK-UCE. (Geoff Ball)

SEASON 1996/1997
Manchester United UEFA Champions League

This season was Manchester United's fifth in the Premier League and again they claimed the title, well ahead of rivals Newcastle United, Arsenal and Liverpool. They would also go as far as reaching the European Cup semi-final, losing to the eventual winners, Borussia Dortmund. Earlier in the group stages, Manchester United had lost at home in Europe for the first time in their history, to Fenerbache of Turkey. Their defence of the FA Cup ended at the fourth round stage, when they lost in a replay to Wimbledon. Their bid for success in the League Cup was also short lived when they were beaten, again in the fourth round to eventual winners Leicester City.

10th September 1996 - Heralded the return of European football to the North West after the events of the summer Euro '96 competition. Manchester United flew out to Turin aboard Star Air B.737-400 F-GRSC (SEU949V), for their first group stage match with Juventus, taking place the following day. Also drawn in United's group were Fenerbache and Rapid Vienna. Three L.1011 Tristar flights chartered today to take travelling fans out to Juventus were Air Atlanta L.1011 TF-ABE (ABD250), Nordic East SE-DPX (ELN701) and Aer Turas EI-TBG (TLA6102), plus Manx Airlines BAe.146 G-MANS (MNX9340), with all aircraft returning in the early hours of the 12th. The game itself produced yet another disappointing trip to Italy, losing 1-0.

25th September 1996 - Two weeks after the Juventus match, Manchester United were at home to Rapid Vienna, who provided several fans charters. The game gave United their first win in the group, beating Rapid Vienna 2-0.

20th November 1996 - The Italians inflicted another home defeat on Manchester United, winning 1-0, and while Juventus were cruising towards qualifications as champions, Manchester United's goal of moving through to the next stage was in serious doubt. As far as the Reds were concerned, everything hung on the final match of the group.

4th December 1996 - Their final group match, away to Rapid Vienna, was one they simply had to win, but not only that, they would only qualify if Juventus beat Fenerbache in the other group match also. With the Italians already qualified, this was no certainty! Manchester United travelled to the match aboard British World BAC 1-11 G-OBWA (BWL7588), with Air Atlanta L.1011 TF-ABH (ABD964) providing the transport for the travelling fans. At the end of the evening, the perfect scenario was achieved! United beat Rapid Vienna 2-0 and Juventus did the Reds a favour by also winning 2-0 at home to Fenerbache. Onwards and upwards!

5th March 1997 - For the knockout phase of the competition, Manchester United were drawn against FC Porto, with the first leg taking place today. The Portuguese team would provide a variety of football charters. The team arrived on the 3rd aboard Air Portugal L.1011-500 CS-TEB at 1613 (TAP9041 from Oporto), which stayed for three days. Two further charters today were Air Portugal A.310 CS-TEX at 1302 (TAP9043 from Lisbon) and Maersk B.737-300 OY-MBN at 1841 (DMA827 from Billund). The latter aircraft brought in Manchester United fans from its Danish branch and on the 4th there was another Air Portugal flight, A.320 CS-TNA (TAP9065 from Oporto).

The day of the match brought in plenty of football related flights. The first to arrive was Ryanair B.737 EI-CJD (RYR5556), with the airline providing many more flights during the day. Appearing were B.737s EI-CJD again (RYR5562), EI-CJH (RYR5568) & EI-CJC (RYR5572) was used for inbound fans. While on the outbound flights were EI-CKR (RYR5579), EI-CJC (RYR5591), EI-CJD (RYR5583) & EI-CJG (RYR5575). Aer Lingus chipped in with Fokker 50 PH-DMO (EIN2214 & B.737-500 EI-CDS (EIN4212) with B.737.500 EI-CDE operating a late evening outbound departure (EIN4219). Air Portugal flights bringing in Portuguese fans were Airbus A.310 CS-TEW at 1153 (TAP9074) & Airbus A.320 CS-TNC at 1058 (TAP9050). A third flight operated by A.320 CS-TNE was due, but it was re-routed to Liverpool due to no slots at Manchester. Two further late evening arrivals were another A.310 CS-TEJ & A.320 CS-TND, both positioning in to take Oporto fans home after seeing their side thoroughly and convincingly beaten by Manchester United 4-0. Two Air Europa Boeing 757s were also used, as well as Air Portugal for the mass influx of Oporto fans, with EC-FTL (AEA501) & EC-GCA (AEA503) both departing after the match. Executive visitors for the match were few and not very exciting: BAe.125 EI-WDC AT 1546, Citation 560 D-CTAN at 1644 and Cessna 414 N414FZ at 1742. Finally, Maersk B.737-300 OY-MAS showed up again, positioning in at 2208 from Oslo to take some of the Danish Reds home. The return match taking place on the 19th March was a mere formality for United. The team flew out the day before aboard Star Air A.320 FGRSD (SEU955V), but despite the tie being virtually over, thousands of fans still made the trip to Portugal on the following aircraft: Monarch Airlines A.300s G-MONR (MON9520) & G-MONS (MON9516), A.320s G-MONY (MON9544) & G-MONZ MON9626) and B.757s G-MONJ (MON9532) & G-MONK (MON9550), Britannia Airways B.767s G-BRIG (BAL864A) & G-OBYD (BAL787A), Leisure International A.320 G-UKLK (LEI9823), Sabre Airways B.727 G-BNNI (SBE294), Air 2000 B.757 G-OOOW (AMM1412), Translift A.300 EI-CJK (TLA513), Caledonian L.1011 G-BBAJ (CKT9842), Air Atlanta L.1011 TF-ABH (ABD985) and European BAC 1-11 G-AXLL (EAF4681). All these flights returned in the early hours of the 20th when Manchester United played a 0-0 draw and advanced to the semi-finals.

7th April 1997 - Man United flew out to Dortmund today aboard Monarch B.757 G-DAJB, with their personnel chartering Star Air A.320 F-GRSD (SEU904L) the following day. Their semi-final first leg match with Borussia Dortmund would be played on the 9th April .The fans flew out on the 8th on four Air 2000 B.757s, two Monarch A.320s and two B.757s, a Leisure Intl A.320, a Britannia Airways B.767 and a Sabre Airways aircraft. These flights operated to destinations such as Cologne, Dusseldorf and Munster, because Dortmund could only handle props. Manchester United lost the match 1-0 with the team returning again on Monarch B.757 G-DAJB in the early hours, with the personnel arriving back on Star Europe B.737-400 F-GRSB (SEU905L from Cologne).

10th April 1997 – Liverpool were also still in the UEFA Cup Winners' Cup, also at the semi-final stage. Air Atlanta L.1011 TF-ABE (ABD728 to Beauvais) flew fans out to

Beauvais for their first-leg match with Paris St. Germain. The return match which took place on the 24th April, also produced a football flight, with the arrival of Air Charter A.300 F-BVGT at 1644 (ACF412 from Paris-CDG). Although Liverpool won their match 2-0, they went out of the competition 3-2 on aggregate.

22nd April 1997 - Hoping to do a little better than Liverpool, Manchester United would play host to the return of Borussia Dortmund. The team arrived today aboard Aero Lloyd A.320 D-ALAD (AEF9220 from Munster), leaving on the 24th. The fans arrived on the 23rd the day of the match on the following flights: on Aero Lloyd MD80 D-ALLO at 1212 (AEF9230 from Munster), Hamburg Air BAe.146 D-AHOI at 1557 (HAS8079 from Paderborn), Lufthansa CRJ D-ACLX at 1154 (DLH5958 from Cologne), Eurowings ATR-42 D-BCRT at 1202 EWG2090 from Dortmund) & Eurowings ATR-72 D-AEWK at 1145 (EWG2094 from Dortmund). The latter two aircraft went straight out again, with another two arriving after the match: ATR-42 D-BCRP (EWG2093 to Munster) & ATR-72 D-AEWI (EWG2097 to Dortmund). A further Aero Lloyd MD80 flight went to Liverpool, again due to slot problems at Manchester. Other flights relating to tonight's match were Cessna 340 D-IBPW, Citation 550 D-IMME, TBM-700 D-FGYY, Aer Lingus B.737-500 EI-CDE (EIN4214) & BAe.146 EI-CLG (EIN2214), CityJet BAe.146 EI-CMS (BCY762), Ryanair B.737s EI-CJE (RRYR5568) & EI-CJG (RYR5572) and BAe.125 EI-WDC, all from Dublin.

13th August 1996 – In a season dominated by Manchester United-related football charters, the only other football flight was today's arrival of Air Truck Navarras ATR-42 EC-GBK at 1334 (TRK036 from Pamplona) making the aircraft's and the airline's only visit. Mainly operated by Air Europa on its inter-island services, it was bringing in Athletico Osasuna to play Stoke City in a friendly, which Stoke won 2-0. (Nik French)

24th September 1996 – OE-LME (AAT4227 from Vienna) brought in the Rapid Vienna team and was the penultimate Austrian Airlines MD80 to visit Manchester. Austrian Airlines also operated scheduled flights between Manchester and Vienna on two occasions, from April 1980 to October 1982, and from October 2001, when they took over the route from Lauda Air, until March 2003. (Denis Norman)

25th September 1996 – Austrian Airlines A.321 OE-LBB (AAT4223 from Vienna) was the first of two fans charters, provided by Rapid Vienna FC. The aircraft was rolled out in this special livery adorned with the portraits of famous Austrians earlier in the year. The images were applied with a special foil, manufactured in Britain. (Geoff Ball)

25th September 1996 - The second football charter today, was Lauda Air B.737-400 OE-LNI (LDA509). The airline operated scheduled flights between Manchester and Vienna, and also Milan briefly, between April 1994 and October 2001 when they were taken over by Austrian Airlines. (Nik French)

28th October 1996 – THY B.737-400 TC-JEI (THY3981 from Istanbul), brought in the Fenerbache team to play Manchester United on the 30th. They returned aboard THY

B.737-400 TC-JDE, having beaten United 1-0. They became the first team to beat the Reds at home in a European game, although two weeks earlier Manchester United did beat the Turkish side 2-0 in Turkey. The airline had got off to a poor start with Manchester. On the 2nd June 1993 they began a twice-weekly service to Istanbul with Boeing 737s, with Airbus A.310s regularly appearing as well, but on the 17th January 1995, they withdrew from the route citing poor passenger loads. However, on the 17th June 1997, they returned and obviously worked a little harder at promoting the route this time round, as eighteen years later they are operating a double daily service. (Denis Norman)

20th November 1996 – The next group game taking place today was Manchester United-Juventus at Old Trafford. The team chose to arrive in Manchester aboard a British Airways Shuttle flight from Heathrow. There was a sole Italian fans' charter, Eurofly Douglas DC-95l I-FLYZ (EEZ1946), which rather curiously didn't arrive from Turin as one would have expected, but from Milan-Malpensa. Other football connected aircraft for the match were EMB-110 LX-SKS, Citations OO-LCM & N7070A and Cessna 414 N414FZ. Fans from Ireland arrived in mass quantities unlike the Italians, with Aer Lingus B.737-500 EI-CDH, Fokker 50 EI-FKD and Ryanair B.737s EI-CKQ, CKR &, CKS all providing transport to/from Manchester. (Nik French)

3rd March 1997 – Air Portugal L.1011-500 CS-TEB (TAP9043 from Oporto) made its first visit, bringing FC Porto into Manchester today. They operated seven Tristar 500s between 1983 and 1997, and CS-TEB was the third and final one to visit. In 2015, it is currently rotting away at Amman after being flown in for storage in 2012. (Nik French)

5th March 1997 – Aer Lingus operated a fleet of six Fokker 50 aircraft in their own right between 1989 and 2001. Despite this PH-DMO seen here, was on its second lease period to the Irish carrier, before returning to Fokker the following month. This aircraft was also the very first production Fokker 50. (Denis Norman)

5th March 1997 – Air Portugal A.310 CS-TEW above and A.320 CS-TNC below made their first visits today. Like THY, Air Portugal had a chequered career at Manchester. They began regular flights way back in 1965 with a summer weekly Lisbon IT flight operated by Constellations. After a fourteen-year gap, regular summer IT flights to Faro began until May 1981. Then a twice-weekly scheduled service to Lisbon began, which lasted until 1984. They had another go at the scheduled market in 1988, operating to Lisbon and Oporto until March 1994. In 2015, they have a scheduled presence at Manchester again, operating up to twice-daily flights to Lisbon. (Both photos Denis Norman)

5th March 1997 – Air Europa B.757s seem to be the staple diet of football charters in the 1990s. Used by the Spanish and the Italians, and on this occasion by Portuguese charters. These aircraft would also be operated by the airline on the many charter flights to/from Manchester. Boeing 757-236 EC-GCA (above) left the fleet later this year. Initially leased to Iberia, it was sold in late 2000. Boeing 757-236 EC-FTL (below) was also sold in late-1997 as N261PW, later operating for Ryan International.
(Above Nik French, below Geoff Ball)

5th March 1997 – Citation 560 D-CTAN seems to visit fairly regularly when significant football matches are played in Manchester. Its last visit was the 9th December 1998 when Bayern Munich came to town, but it was sold the following March. (Denis Norman)

23rd April 1997 – Bringing in Borussia Dortmund fans, was Aero Lloyd MD80 D-ALLO on its first visit. The airline which was founded in 1980, initially operated with three SE.210 Caravelles. In 1988 they expanded their operations to cover scheduled services, including flights to Paris, Zurich and London, but four years these were later dropped. The airline ceased operations in October 2003 after shareholders refused to continue to fund the airline. (Nik French)

23rd April 1997 – D-AHOI was the last of three Hamburg Airlines BAe.146-300s visiting during 1996-1997. Amidst the backdrop of work taking place on the main terminal, this aircraft was purchased by Eurowings after Hamburg Air's demise, who operated it until 2010. Currently registered as ZS-SOP, it is stored at Lanseria, South Africa. (Nik French)

23rd April 1997 – Despite it being a European Cup semi-final, the number of football charters provided by the Germans was disappointing, although it did produce four Eurowings flights, all of which were first visits. The first of two ATR-72s was D-AEWK, seen here on short finals. This aircraft went straight out, with the return flight being operated by D-AEWI which positioned in at 2211. (Denis Norman)

23rd April 1997 – In a similar operation to their ATR-72s, once ATR-42 D-BCRT had dropped off its passengers, it departed empty back to Dortmund. A second ATR-42, D-BCRP arrived at 2314 for the return flight. Both aircraft were first visits. (Nik French)

23rd April 1997 – Just like Citation 560 D-CTAN, D-IMME also appeared when European football was played at Old Trafford. Although Citation 550 D-IMME is still registered as such, it made its last visit on 20th February 2008. (Denis Norman)

SEASON 1997/1998
Manchester United UEFA Champions League

Local aviation enthusiasts now had to rely purely on Manchester United for providing European football charters. Interestingly, key domestic matches at Old Trafford were also attracting increasing numbers of executive aircraft, particularly when Chelsea or Arsenal were in town. As far as the 1997-1998 season was concerned, it would end in a fairly disastrous fashion. Having opened up an eleven-point gap by March, and still in contention for a League and European double, they were pipped to the Premier League title by Arsenal, who managed a nine-match winning streak in the last two months of the season. They were beaten in the fifth round of the FA Cup by Barnsley and dumped out of the Champions League by AS Monaco at the quarter-final stage. This was Manchester United's first trophy-less season since 1994-95.

16th September 1997 - Star Europe A.320 F-GRSE (SEU954L) was chartered to take Manchester United to Poland for their first European group match, taking place against Kosice the following evening. Two fans' charters on the 17th were provided by European Airlines BAC 1-11 G-AVMZ (EAF4696) and British World BAC 1-11 G-OBWA (BWL7827). The Polish side were convincingly beaten 3-0, but United would not have it so easy for their next match in two weeks, when their opponents would be the Italian side, Juventus.

30th September 1997 - Eurofly MD-83 EI-CMM (EEZ1910 from Turin) was chartered to bring the Juventus team to Manchester. The following day there was a small selection of charters in conjunction with the match taking place later that evening. The only Italian fans' charter was provided by another Eurofly MD83 visit, EI-CNR (EEZ1988 from Bergamo). German Citation 525 D-IRKE and Beech 200 N8PY both arrived from Cologne and Ronaldsway respectively. Irish visitors for the match were CityJet BAe.146 EI-CMY (BCY736), Aer Lingus B.737-400 EI-BXA (EIN2216) & PA-31 Navajo EI-CNM, all arriving from Dublin. In one of the best European games that Manchester United had been involved in, they beat Juventus 3-2 and now had two wins out of two.

21st October 1997 -   With things looking good in the Champions League, Feyenoord were United's next opponents. The Dutch team arrived today on Ratioflug Fokker F.27 D-ADUP at 1159 (RAT027 from Rotterdam). The following day, match day, the Dutch supporters arrived in considerably more numbers than the Italians previously, chartering Corse Air B.747 F-GPJM (CRL832), Transavia B.737-300 PH-TSZ (TRA8349) and Tulip Air Beech 200 PH-ATM (TL9A). Others included Citation 560 C-CTAN, PA-31 Navajo N9210Y and Jetair Metroliner OY-JEO (BDI1603). Irish support for Manchester United was provided by Ryanair B.737 EI-CKQ (RYR5568), Aer Lingus B.737-500 (EIN2216) & PA-31 Navajo EI-CNM (RDK029).

4th November 1997 - The Manchester United European bandwagon rolled on unabated! Having beaten Feyenoord 2-1 at home in October, they flew out to Rotterdam today aboard Air Holland B.737-300 PH-OZB (AHR813), and this time won 3-1. The game took place the following day with the fans flying out exclusively on Monarch Airlines

A.300 G-OJMR (MON9270), A.320 G-MONW (MON9250) & B.757 G-MOND (MON9256).

27ᵗʰ November 1997 - Manchester United were now virtually guaranteed to be in the next round with a maximum of twelve points from four games. Next it was the turn of the Slovakian side Kosice to come to Old Trafford to try their luck. The team arrived today aboard Tupolev TU-154 OM-BYO at 1044 (EAT4465 from Kosice). A further fans' flight arriving the following day operated by Air Transport Europe was Tupolev TU-134 OM-GAT at 1045 (EAT4467 from Kosice). The only other aircraft to arrive in connection with the match were BAe.125 EI-WDC, Cessna 414 G-AZFZ from Jersey and Denim Air Fokker 50 PH-DMO (EIN2202 from Dublin). The Slovaks provided very little resistance and were easily beaten 3-0. Manchester United was now through to the quarter-finals with one match remaining, away to Juventus in two weeks time.

10ᵗʰ December 1997 - On another grey morning, Manchester United flew out to Turin for the final group match aboard Air 2000 B.757 G-OOOW (AMM9160). Again the fans travelled in larger numbers than they really needed to, as they knew their team had already qualified for the next stage. Aircraft charters were provided by Monarch Airlines A.300 G-MONS (MON9254) and A.320s G-MONW (MON926A) & G-MONX (MON9370), Airtours B.757 G-CSVS (AIH3747) and finally Leisure International A.320 G-UKLK (LEI9050). Although Manchester United effectively had nothing to play for, Juventus certainly did, because victory would ensure the Italians qualified for the next round as runners up, which they managed to achieve beating United 1-0.

3ʳᵈ March 1998 - Manchester United's quarter-final opponents would be as Monaco, with the Reds travelling to Nice on European BAC 1-11 G-AVMY (EAF4948), ahead of the match being played the following evening. Amongst the various football charters to Nice on the match day itself (4ᵗʰ) were Translift A.300 EI-TLL (TLA157) and Maersk Fokker 50 OY-MMG (DMA1923), the latter aircraft with United fans from Denmark. After achieving a 0-0 draw, hopes must have been high that United could do the business on home turf and progress to another European semi-final.

17ᵗʰ March 1998 - Today saw the arrival of the AS Monaco team and officials aboard Star Europe A.320 F-GRSE (SEU975L from Nice), staying until the 19ᵗʰ. All the main activity took place the following day, or that should have been the case! There was only one fans' charter flight, Air Charter A.320 F-GLGM (ACF397V). This flight had originally diverted to Leeds due to a three hour closure during the day after ATP G-MANG suffered a nosewheel collapse on landing. Executive visitors were only slightly more interesting, producing BAe.125 F-GJDE, Beech 90 3A-MON, Falcon 20 F-GYSL and Learjet 45 D-CDEN. The Irish visitors however were numerous with Aer Lingus BAe.146s EI-CLG (EIN4214) & EI-CLY (EIN4218) and B.737-500s EI-CDB (EIN2216) & EI-CDE (EIN2202), Ryanair B.737s EI-CJC (RYR5568), EI-CNY (RYR5532), EI-CNZ (RYR5578) & EI-COB (RYR5546). Mention should also be made of the visit of Keenair EMB-110 G-BGYT (JFK590 from Gloucester-Staverton). It arrived with a load of Irish supporters for the Manchester United match, who had previously been at the Gold Cup meeting at Cheltenham. They would return (or so they thought) after the match back to Staverton, but they had to fly into Birmingham instead due to Staverton closing for the evening. The game itself resulted in a 1-1 draw, meaning Monaco went through to the Semi-finals on away goals. The real irony was that Juventus, who finished second in the same group as United, made it all the way to the final, losing 1-0 to Real Madrid.

5th August 1997 – Immaculate looking Czech Government TU-154 OK-BYZ (CIE012 from Prague) is seen making its only visit to Manchester, bringing in Slavia Prague for a pre-season match with Manchester United. This was the second friendly to be held at Old Trafford inside of a week. On the 30th July, Inter Milan arrived aboard Eurofly MD83 EI-CEK. In 1998 TU-154 OK-BYZ was transferred to the Czech Air Force, and served for a further six years, but since 2008 it has been stored at Kbely, the site of Prague's original airport. (Nik French)

17th September 1997 – Two classic BAC 1-11s were used to ferry Manchester United fans out for their match with Kosice that evening. European example G-AVMT, formerly operated by BEA/British Airways for twenty-three years, operated for a further six years before being withdrawn in 2003. It made its last visit to Manchester on the 17th May 2001, operating a charter from/to Biarritz. British World BAC 1-11 G-OBWA, formerly Dan-Air G-BDAT, was picked up by the charter airline in 1992 after Dan-Air went bankrupt. British World themselves ceased trading in December 2001 and G-OBWA was subsequently scrapped. (Above Allan Jones, below Nik French)

1st October 1997 – Eurofly MD83 EI-CNR, seen here about to be repositioned onto the Western Apron, was a first visit to Manchester. The airline's fleet of MD80s would eventually be superseded by Airbus A.320s, most having been sold in 2001. This aircraft, EI-CNR, was sold to Luxor Air in 2002 as SU-BMF and currently operates for Falcon Air Express as N307FA. (Nik French)

1st October 1997 – Citation 525 D-IRKE was actually delivered through Manchester on the 13th January 1996. Although still German-registered, it made its last visit to Manchester way back on the 30th October 2001. (Denis Norman)

21st October 1997 – Since its last visit in June 1996, Ratioflug Fokker F.27 D-ADUP had been transformed from a basically all white livery, into a rather fetching blue and white colour scheme. It had arrived with Feyenoord FC and stayed for two days. (Nik French)

22nd October 1997 – By 1997, French airline Corse Air were operating four second-hand Boeing 747-200s. The third of these to visit Manchester was F-GPJM. All aircraft were operated in a high-capacity configuration, and this flight arrived with 515 Feyenoord supporters! As the airline began to replace their older -200 series with -400s, F-GPJM became surplus to requirement and withdrawn in September 2001. (Nik French)

22nd October 1997 – Transavia B.737-300 PH-TSZ (TRA8349) was a further Feyenoord football charter, seen here on the western apron on a cold but sunny day. (Nik French)

22nd October 1997 – Another smart looking aircraft to arrive today was Tulip Air Beech 200 PH-ATM. This Dutch charter company operated PH-ATM from 1994 until 2004, when it was sold in Germany after the company ceased operating its own aircraft. In 2015, Tulip Air still trades, but now specializes in offering potential owners assistance in aircraft acquisition. (Nik French)

26ᵗʰ November 1997 – Slovak Government TU-154 OM-BYO arrived with the Kosice team and stayed for two days. This aircraft had visited back in 1992, operating a scheduled flight for CSA as OK-BYO, when it was a Czech government machine. Now twenty-five years old, it still flies for the Slovak Government. (Lee Collins)

27ᵗʰ November 1997 – Built in 1976 and delivered to Aeroflot as CCCP-65034, TU-134 OM-GAT was leased to Air Transport Europe between 1995 and 2000, and today was its one and only visit to Manchester. In 2006, it was purchased by Aeroflot (again) as RA-65034 and made it into the airline's new and most recent colour scheme. However by 2010, it was reported as withdrawn. (Lee Collins)

17th March 1998 – Star Europe A.320 F-GRSE was one of six aircraft operated by the French airline that visited Manchester between 1997 and 2002. It was formed in 1995 and later became XL Airways France, part of the XL Airways group. The group went bankrupt on 12th September 2008, but was saved when it was purchased by an investment bank on the same day. (Nik French)

18th March 1998 – Learjet 55 D-CDEN is seen being repositioned from the NEA apron, having just dropped off its passengers, for overnight parking opposite the viewing park, a parking area locally known as the 'Romper', after the nearby pub! (Denis Norman)

SEASON 1998/1999
Manchester United UEFA Champions League

The 1998–99 season was the most successful in the history of Manchester United. After finishing the previous season without winning any titles, United won a treble of trophies (the Premier League, FA Cup and UEFA Champions League), the first side in English football to achieve such a feat. During the campaign, United lost only five times, including a one-off Charity Shield fixture against eventual winners Tottenham Hotspur and their only home defeat, a league match against Middlesbrough in December 1998. A run of thirty-three games unbeaten in all competitions began on 26th December 1998 at home to Nottingham Forest, with the culmination of this historic season was the comeback against Bayern Munich in the Champions League final. By the end of the season, they had become the world's richest football club and the most valuable sporting brand worldwide.

25th August 1998 - Manchester United entered this season's UEFA Champions League by way of runners-up in the Premier League. Their potential passage was a little harder this time, by having to enter the competition in the second Qualifying Round stage. Their first opponents were Polish side LKS Lodz and the first leg was played at Old Trafford two weeks earlier, with United winning 2-0. For the second leg, they flew out today aboard Titan BAe.146 G-ZAPK (AWC327A to Lodz) where they managed a 0-0 stalemate. This aggregate score of 2-0 put Manchester United through into the group phase, along with Brondby, Barcelona and Bayern Munich, an extremely tough group.

14th September 1998 - Iberia A.320 EC-FDB (IBE4038 from Barcelona) dropped Barcelona FC off two days ahead of their match with Manchester United. Air Europa B.737-400 EC-FZZ (AEA818) arrived at 2312 on the 16th to pick the team up after the match, which ended 3-3. Other flights on the 16th in connection with the game were Ryanair B.737s EI-CNZ (RYR5568 & RYR5578) & EI-CNT (RYR5578), Aer Lingus B.737-400 EI-BXK (EIN2216) plus Beech 350 EI-CRI and Cessna 414 N414FZ.

29th September 1998 - British Midland B.737-400 G-OBMO (BMA6421) was Manchester United's transport for their match with Bayern Munich. The fans' charters took place the following day utilising the following aircraft: Air Scandic A.300 G-TTMC (SCY731), Leisure Intl A.321 G-UNIE (LEI9412), Monarch Airlines B.757 G-MOND (MON8133) and another British Midland B.737, G-BVKC (BMA8222).

21st October 1998 - After gaining another valuable point away to Bayern Munich, Manchester United finally got into their stride by beating Danish side Brondby 6-2 away from home. The team travelled on the 20th aboard Monarch A.320 G-OZBA (MON8134), while the supporters flew today on Leisure Intl A.320 G-UKLL (LEI9346), Air 2000 A.321 G-OOAE (LEI9372) & Monarch B.757 G-MONB (MON8134)

3rd November 1998 - Although not a big club but seemingly well supported, the Brondby team and officials arrived this morning on two flights, Maersk B.737-700s OY-MRB at 1039 (DMA809) & OY-MRC (DMA825) at 1053, both from Copenhagen. The football charters continued the following day with another pair of Danish B.737s, this time Sterling B.737-800s OY-SEB (SNB1611) at 0923 & OY-SEE at 0944 (SNB1595), Premiair A.320 OY-CNB at 0921 (VKG4063), Aer Lingus BAe.146 EI-CSL (EIN2216) and the lighter side were represented by Cessna 414 N414FZ & PA-31 Navajo EI-CNM. Despite all this support, the Danish side were again soundly beaten, this time 5-0.

24th November 1998 - This season's European adventure was going well so far, eight points in the group and unbeaten with the latest match being Barcelona away. A new airline to Manchester used to fly the team was AB Airlines when B.737-400 G-OABL (AZX454) positioned in from Gatwick on its first visit, while the exodus of fans left today and the following day aboard Monarch B.757s G-DAJB (MON9162 & MON9200) & G-MONE (also twice – MON9174 & MON9214), Air 2000 B.757 G-OOOU (AM9394) and Translift A.300s EI-TLB (TLA940) & EI-TLM (TLA938).

8th December 1998 - Hapag-Lloyd A.310 D-AHLB (HLF973 from Munich) was the aircraft of choice to bring Bayern Munich to Manchester, leaving empty for Hanover later in the afternoon. This flight was also carrying a number of fans, but surprisingly there were no further charters from Germany, possibly because the German fans realised they were through to the next round anyway. On the 10th, another Hapag-Lloyd A.310, D-AHLC (HLF974), arrived to take the German side home.

9th December 1998 - The football-related flights for this evening's match were almost exclusively for Manchester United's Irish contingent, all arriving from Dublin: Ryanair B.737s EI-CJE (RYR5568), EI-CNT (RYR5582), EI-COB (RYR5564 & RYR5566) & EI-COX (RYR5562 & RYR5578), Aer Lingus B.737s EI-BXB (EIN3204), EI-BXI (EIN3210), EI-CDG (EIN3202), EI-CDS (EIN2206) & BAe.146 EI-CLG (EIN2218). The lighter side included Citation 550 N7070A at 1636, Gulfstream V EI-WGV at 1640, BAe.125 EI-COV at 1710 and Cessna 414 N414FZ at 1827. Finally, there was a solitary German executive visitor, regular Citation 560 D-CTAN at 1719 (from Buchel). The game ended in a 1-1 draw that meant both teams had qualified for the Quarter Finals. Manchester United had finished second in the group, but undefeated, one point behind Bayern Munich. A Condor B.767 was due to arrive after the match to pick up some Bayern Munich fans, but it went to Liverpool instead due to night time closures at MAN.

2nd March 1999 - It was generally recognised that Italian supporters showed little inclination for following their side until the final stages, and with Manchester United drawn to play Inter-Milan in the Quarter finals, with the first leg being be played at Old Trafford, this indeed proved to be the case. The team arrived today in style aboard Alitalia MD-11 I-DUPD, which arrived at 1405 (AZA8206 from Milan). The arrival at 1916 of Falcon 900 I-BEAU (from Milan-Linate) was also football-connected, bringing in their Brazilian forward, Ronaldo. This aircraft also positioned in after the match and night-stopped, before returning to Italy with Ronaldo, who was obviously too good to travel with the rest of the team!

3rd March 1999 - Match day brought a major influx of football charters, bringing Inter and United supporters alike. Air Europe Italy B.767-300 EI-CJA made two visits from Milan (AEL5108 & AEL5198), the second return flight left after the match while a further aircraft, I-AIMQ (AEL5199), also arrived after the match to take supporters home. Eurofly provided three MD83 charters, EI-CMZ (EEZ1962), EI-CMM (EEZ1974) & EI-CPB (EEZ1938), which now wears full Alitalia colours. Supporters from Southern Ireland again travelled in vast numbers, and provided the following: Aer Lingus BAe.146 EI-CLY

(EIN3208), B.737s EI-BXC (EIN3210 & EIN3214) & EI-CDE (EIN3216) and Ryanair B.737s EI-CJH (RYR5562), EI-CNT (RYR5578), EI-CNY (RYR5568 & RYR5574), EI-COX (RYR5564 & RYR5582). Executive visitors were Citation 560 G-CZAR at 1328, Citation 550 N800LA at 1401, Citation 525 at 1532, Cessna 414 N414FZ at 1835 and Falcon 20 HB VKO at 1727 (FPG663 from Geneva).

4th March 1999 - Alitalia MD11 I-DUPU arrived at 1005 (AZA8206) to collect the beaten Inter Milan side. Having lost 2-0, it was looking like the Italian side's European exit was inevitable, as they needed to beat United by three goals in the return leg.

16th March 1999 - Barring any disasters, the progression of Manchester United into the semi-finals was just a formality. The team travelled to Milan today on Sabre Airways B.737-800 G-OJSW (SBE4124), returning in the early hours of the 18th. There were also the following fans' charters: Translift A.300 EI-CJK (TLA128), Air Atlanta L.1011 TF-ABE (KGC5438), Caledonian L.1011 G-BBAE (TLA142) and Monarch Airlines A.320 G-OZBA (MON955A).

17th March 1999 - Match day itself provided further fans charters: Monarch Airlines A.321 G-OZBC (MON9560) and B.757s G-DAJB (MON9546), G-MOND (MON9603) & G-MONK (MON9522), Air 2000 B.767-300 G-OOAN (AMM9608) and Britannia B.767 G-BRIG (BAL864A). There were no nasty surprises on the night, the result being a 1-1 draw, and United now went through to face more Italian competition, this time Juventus.

6th April 1999 - The first leg of the European Champions League semi-final between Manchester and Juventus would be played at Old Trafford. The Juventus team and officials arrived today aboard Air Europe Italy B.767-300 EI-CJA (AEL5822 from Turin), positioning out later to Rome-FCO.

7th April 1999 - Match day generated a fair number of executive visitors, but football fans charters were a little disappointing, considering it was a semi-final. The first football-related flight was Hawker 800 LX-GBY and others during the day were Learjets OO-LFS & I-DLON, BAe.125 EI-WDC, Falcon 10 OE-GSC, Falcon 20 PH-OMC, Falcon 50 F-GOAL, Citation 550 G-OEJA, Cessna 414 N414FZ & PA-31 EI-CNM. Bringing Italian fans to Manchester were Air Europe Italy B.767-300 EI-CNS at 1055 (AEL5828) and Eurofly MD80s EI-CMM at 1245 (EEZ1970) & EI-CNR at 1537 (EEZ1926) all from Milan-Malpensa and also Monarch A.330 G-SMAN at 1421 (MON919 from Shannon) & Aer Lingus A.330 EI-DUB. Arriving after the match to collect the Italian team and fans respectively were Air Europe Italy B.767-300s EI-CJA (AEL5823) & EI-CLS (AEL5829), who must have been delighted after their side gained an impressive 1-1 draw at Old Trafford.

11th April 1999 – In between European games, Old Trafford played host to another semi-final, a FA Cup game between Tottenham Hotspur and Newcastle. Spurs travelled up for the match on Titan Airways BAe.146 G-ZAPK (AWC720 from Stansted), while Newcastle arrived aboard Gill Airways ATR-42 G-BVJP (GIL134M from Newcastle).

20th April 1999 – After the stalemate in the first leg, qualification to the European Cup Final, which would have been their first in thirty-one years, was looking extremely slim. Manchester United travelled out today to Turin aboard Monarch Airlines B.757 G-

MONB (MON966A) with the fans making the trip the following day aboard Air 2000 A.321s G-OOAF (AMM9524) & G-OOAH (AMM9446), Air Atlanta L.1011s TF-ABU (MON9710) & TF-ABE (CKT9154), G-OOAH (AMM9446), Sabre Airways B.737-800 G-OJSW (SBE4186), Airtours B.767-300 G-SJMC (AIH6723) and Monarch Airlines B.757 G-MONK (MON9696). Those that made the trip witnessed the impossible, United finally winning a match on Italian soil, the result was an incredible 3-2 victory and a place in the European Cup Final for the first time since those heady days in 1968.

24th May 1999 - With the European Final taking place in Barcelona on the 26th, Manchester United flew out today aboard Sabre Airways B.737-800 G-OJSW (SBE756). What followed was a massive airlift of fans using 55 flights, which took up 255 extra movements, as many aircraft positioned in and out too. Despite some ticket problems, such as those not having any match tickets and sometimes flight tickets as well, everything went relatively smoothly and ATC did a fine job. Numerous foreign aircraft were used, as well as some locally based aircraft: Sabre Airways B.727 G-BNNI (24th/27th) and B.737-800s G-OJSW (24th/25th/27th) & G-OKDN (24th), Monarch A.320 G-MONW (24th/25th), Boeing 757s G-MOND (25th), G-MONK (26th/27th), A.300 OJMR (25th), A.330 EOMA (26th/27th), DC-10 G-DMCA (26th/27th), Air Scandic L-1011 EI-CNN (25th/26th/27th) & A.300 G-SWJW (25th/26th/27th/28th), Caledonian L-1011s G-BBAH (26th), TF-ABM (26th), Britannia Airways B.767 G-BYAA (26th), Airtours DC-10 G-BYDA (26th/27th) and finally Titan Airways BAe.146 G–ZAPK (26th/27th) and ATR-42 G-BUPS, which took out a party of disabled fans to watch the game.

As if this wasn't enough, there were many foreigners, which produced numerous first time visitors (*). Transair were probably the biggest operator, producing A.300s EI-CJK (24th/26th/27th/28th), EI-TLK (25th/26th/27th) & EI-TLM (25th/26th/27th), whilst German based A.320 EI-TLS was present on the 26th/27th, as was EI-TLT* which carried Air Andalus titles. Running a close second for flights operated during this four day period was Corsair with their high-capacity aircraft, B.747-300s F-GSUN* (25th/26th/27th/28th), F-GSEA (26th/27th), B.747-200* F-GLNA (25th/26th/27th) and B.747SP F-GTOM* (25th/26th), plus two B.737s, -300 F-GFUI (26th/27th) & -400 EC-GUI (26th/27th), which all operated several flights each day. Balair A.310 HB-IPL was used extensively (24th/25th/26th/27th/28th), whilst Constellation A.320 OO-COH was also present (25th/27th). Operating just a single rotation on each day was Aero Lyon DC-10 F-BTDD (25th/27th), Virgin Express B.737 OO-VJO (26th/27th), Air Liberte DC-10 F-GPVD (26th/27th), Air Atlanta B.747s TF-ABG (26th/27th) & TF-ABY* (26th/27th), with the latter in basic old Saudia colours; Star Europe A.320 F-GRSH* (26th/27th) & L.1011 C-FTSW* (26th/27th), as was Aeris (ex Air Toulouse) B.737 FGHXK. Some of the Spanish carriers also involved were Spanair MD-83 EC-HBP* (27th) and EC-GXU (26th), Iberworld A.320 EC-GZE (26th/27th) and Futura B.737-400s EC-GRX (27th), ECH-CN (26th) and EC-HCP (26/7). The sum total of all this was an uplift of around 16,000 fans, who saw another fantastic European adventure end in victory over Bayern Munich 2-1.

29th September 1998 – The long road to the Champions League final for Manchester United began today, when British Midland B.737-400 G-OBMO, which had been based during the summer operating for Air 2000, flew out the team and officials to Germany for their first match in the tournament, against Bayern Munich. (Nik French)

3rd November 1998 – Parked under the brightening skies, are Maersk 737-700s OY-MRB & OY-MRC, which had arrived earlier this morning, within fifteen minutes of each other, bringing in the Brondby FC team, officials, and a few Danish fans. (Nik French)

4th November 1998 – Danish operator Sterling made their first visit to Manchester today, operating their new fleet of Boeing 737s. B.737-300 OY-SEE, seen here shortly after arrival on a damp, wet morning, was making its only visit as such, although it had been in previously as EC-245 & EC-ENT for Hispania. (Denis Norman)

4th November 1998 – Wearing the airline's smart new livery, the second Sterling B.737 to visit today was B.737-800 OY-SEB, which was its only visit to Ringway. It would be another eight years before the airline would be seen again at Manchester, operating a number of football flights in October 2006. However, exactly two years later in 2008, the airline declared bankruptcy and ceased flying after forty-six years. (Nik French)

4th November 1998 – Yet another aircraft today bringing in Brondby fans, was the first visit of Premiair A.320 OY-CNB. Re-branded within the MyTravel group in 2002, this was the second of eight Premiair A.320s to visit from 1996-2001, primarily for maintenance at FLS. (Nik French)

9th December 1998 – During the 1990s, Ryanair were the main transport for Irish supporters coming over from Dublin to watch Manchester United at Old Trafford. B.737-200 EI-CJE, sporting special 'Jaguar' colours and titles, has just arrived on one such flight, bringing fans for the match between Man U and Bayern Munich. (Allan Jones)

2nd March 1999 – Alitalia MD11 I-DUPD brought in the mighty Inter Milan team to Manchester, on a wet and miserable morning. This magnificent machine was the first of two Alitalia MD11s in connection with this match. The airline operated eight aircraft from 1991-2003, with I-DUPD operating their very last MD11 flight on 1st December 2003. Eventually purchased by Lufthansa Cargo as D-ALCD, it was operated until January 2015. (Stuart Prince)

3rd March 1999 – After Northern Executive acquired their first Learjet with the prestigious registration G-LEAR in 1979, G-LJET could be considered the second. Registered in 1988, it became a fairly regular visitor to Manchester and at the time of today's visit, it was operated by Farnborough-based Gama Aviation until 2003 when it was sold as N643MJ. (Denis Norman)

4ᵗʰ March 1999 – Falcon 900 I-BEAU from Milan-Linate had night-stopped from the previous evening. It would fly Inter's star Brazilian centre-forward Ronaldo back to Milan later today. Sixteen years later, it is still operated as I-BEAU, although its last visit to Manchester was back in March 2009. (Nik French)

4ᵗʰ March 1999 – On slightly better day weather wise, Alitalia MD11 I-DUPU arrived to collect Inter Milan after their defeat last night. After being withdrawn as a passenger aircraft, from 2006-2009 it was used as pure cargo aircraft by Alitalia, registered as EI-UPU. In 2015, it is being operated by Centurion Cargo as N985AR. (Stuart Prince)

16th March 1999 – Manchester United used Sabre Airways B.737-800s on several occasions as transport during 1999. G-OJSW seen departing for Milan with the United team, was one of four operated by the airline prior to becoming Excel Airways when in late 2000, the Libra Holiday Group purchased a majority share. (Allan Jones)

6th April 1999 – Making its first visit today, in connection with the Man United-Juventus match, was Abelag Aviation Learjet 45 OO-LFS This Belgian charter company had been existence since 1964, operating a wide range of aircraft including a Boeing 707, OO-ABA, during 1979/80. As well as undertaking ad hoc charter, air taxi, cargo, medical and helicopter VIP flights, they also maintain and handle aircraft. In May 2010, Abelag received "the Gold Safety Flight Award" from the European Business Aviation Association, for more than 40 years of safe flights around the world. (Allan Jones)

25th May 1999 – Constellation A.320 OO-COH was one of several interesting visitors over the next few days uplifting Manchester United fans to Barcelona. Founded in June 1995, this short-lived Belgian airline initially operated two Boeing 727s, which were later replaced by three new Airbus A.320s, making them the first Benelux country to operate the Airbus A.320 family. Their market was mainly holiday flights, and they made their first visit to Manchester on the 12th September 1996 with B.727 OO-CAH. However, by the 3rd December 1999, after financial difficulties, they ceased operations and were declared bankrupt on the 15th December 1999. (Allan Jones)

25th May 1999 – Balair Airbus A.310 HB-IPL would make six round trips to Barcelona over the next few days. This aircraft was also an occasional visitor on fuel stops en-route to/from North America, originating from Zurich. Balair/CTA ceased trading in 2001 when the Swissair Group collapsed, as they were the majority shareholder. They re-emerged in late 2001 as Belair, and are now part of the Air Berlin group. (Lee Collins)

26th May 1999 – Although the European Cup Final was being played at Barcelona, not all flights operated into there, as a significant number also operated into Gerona. Virgin Express B.737-400 OO-VJO was one such flight (VEX5322), having positioned initially from Paris-CDG. It returned from Gerona the following morning (VEX5323) with jubilant United fans, who witnessed yet another classic European match! (Denis Norman)

26th May 1999 – Air Toulouse International B.737-200 F-GHXK also arrived early, this time from Nantes, to operate outbound to Gerona (TLE233), before returning the following morning (TLE234). Now wearing their smart new tail colours, the airline was renamed Aeris later in the year and F-GHXK operated for a further two years before being purchased by Nigerian airline Bellview. (Geoff Ball)

26th May 1999 – One of the more unusual airlines used for the airlift was Canadian airline Air Transat. This fine-looking Tristar 500, C-FTSW, operated one round trip to Gerona (SEU910L/911L), before positioning out to Paris-CDG. Formerly CS-TEF with Air Portugal, it was operated by Air Transat until July 2004. It last flew with Kallat Elsaker Air as XT-RAD in 2008, and is said to be currently stored at Sabha, Libya. (Denis Norman)

26th May 1999 - TF-ABG arrived from Manston the previous evening and left today on a round trip to Barcelona (ABD505/6). Air Atlanta had built a fleet of second-hand L.1011 Tristars & Boeing 747s, TF-ABG seen here, operated for Air Atlanta for a relatively short time between March 1998 and September 1999. Its final appearance at Manchester took place on the 27th September 1999. (Nik French)

26ᵗʰ May 1999 – One of various Corsair aircraft performing footballing duties was B.747-200 F-GLNA, seen here positioning from Paris-Orly to operate the first of several flights to Barcelona. Making its first visit today, despite being in service since 1992, F-GLNA was withdrawn during 2000 and broken up in March 2003. (Denis Norman)

26ᵗʰ May 1999 – Corsair B.737-300 F-GFUI was another one of the French airlines aircraft employed on Spanish shuttle duties. The airline operated up to eight Boeing 737-300/400s, including leased Futura B.737-400 EC-GUI, which was also present during the fans' exodus to Barcelona and Gerona. (Terry Shone)

26th May 1999 – A general shot of Terminal 2 during the morning, busy with scheduled, charter and football flights alike. (Mark White)

26th May 1999 – Possibly the best of the Corsair B.747s during these few days, was the visit of their sole B.747SP, F-GTOM. This was the sixth of eight of these unique 'Special Performance' variations on the standard Boeing 747 to visit Manchester. It would continue making occasional appearances until 2002, when it made an incredible twelve visits, all sub-charters for Britannia Airways. On 17th September 2002, it made its final flight from Paris-Orly to Chateauroux for storage, taking a mere 29 minutes. (Nik French)

25th May 1999 – Beside F-GLNA, another Corsair B.747 making its first visit was this - 300 series, F-GSUN. Although it would continue to make occasional appearances until 2001, it was sold to Air Atlanta as TF-AMJ when Corsair replaced their B.747-200/300s with slightly newer B.747-400s. (Lee Collins)

27th May 1999 – Another Air Atlanta B.747 used during this period was TF-ABY, seen landing back at Manchester (ABD511 from Barcelona), having made its first appearance two days earlier. These were the only visits of this aircraft to Manchester, spending most of its two years with Air Atlanta leased ether to Iberia or Saudia, before arriving at Marana for storage in September 1999. (Denis Norman)

SEASON 1999/2000
Manchester United UEFA Champions League
Leeds United UEFA Cup

Was anything going to top last season for Manchester United? Well, they won the Premier League for the sixth time in eight seasons, which they achieved with a record 18 point margin and 97 goals scored, but they surrendered their European Cup title to eventual champions Real Madrid in the quarter-finals. The club controversially did not defend their FA Cup crown, upon request by the Football Association. They were asked to compete in the inaugural FIFA Club Championship in Brazil instead.

13th September 1999 - Croatia Zagreb were the first opponents for the defending European champions, arriving today aboard Croatian A.319 9A-CTH at 1353 (CTN1586 from Zagreb). As it was so early in the season, the game attracted few connected flights. The game was played the following evening with two fans' charters arriving earlier in the day: Adria Airways A.320 S5-AAC (ADR3654/5 from/to Ljubljana), Croatian A.319 9A-CTG (CTN4528/9 from/to Zagreb) and for United's Irish fans, Aer Lingus B.737-500 EI-CDB (EIN2208/9). There were just two executive flights, both regulars, with BAe.125 EI-WDC & PA-31 EI-CNM. The Croatia Zagreb team left Manchester on the 15th when another Croatian A.319, 9A-CTG arrived, departing to Zagreb as CTN4587. The game itself was an extremely disappointing 0-0 draw, but the following week United got back to their winning ways by beating Austrian side Sturm Graz away from home 3-0.

28th September 1999 - United's third group match would take place the following evening against Marseille, who arrived today aboard Air Toulouse B.737-300 F-GNFC (TLE278), taking them home two days later having been beaten 2-1. The match day did not produce many more football charters than United's last home match, but it did bring in more fans! Corsair produced two of its 'sardine-can' B.747s, -300 F-GSEA at 1040 (CRL850) & -200 F-GLNA (CRL852), also Virgin Express B.737-400 OO-VJO at 1217 (VEX5322) and Aer Lingus B.737-400 EI-BXI (EIN2218/9) with the only executive visitor again being PA-31 EI-CNM.

19th October 1999 -   Manchester United's only defeat in the group took place today in the hands of Marseille, who got their revenge from three weeks earlier by winning 1-0. The team flew out on the 18th on Sabre Airways B.737-80 G-OJSW (SBE7221) with just two fans' flights, Air 2000 B.757 G-OOOU (AMM890C) & European BAC 1-11 G-AVMZ (EAF6682). At this point it seemed that United would qualify for the next phase, but as winners or runners-up of the group was unclear at this stage.

20th October 1999 - A change from all the Man United-related football traffic, this evening saw the arrival at 1035 of AviaExpress Tupolev TU-154 RA-85636, bringing in Lokomotiv Moscow for a UEFA Cup match the following evening with Leeds United.

27th October 1999 - Passage into the next group stage was guaranteed today, when Manchester United beat Croatia Zagreb 2-1 away. The team flew out to Croatia the previous morning aboard Air 2000 G-OOAF (AMM892C). The fans showed little interest in this match, despite its significance, with just two charters being enough for the die-hards: Air 2000 A.321 G-OOAJ operating two flights (AMM956C & AMM984C). Those travelling were rewarded with the knowledge that victory ensured United as the champions of the group.

2nd November 1999 - The final group match would be played at home against Sturm Graz. The team and officials arrived aboard Austrian Airlines MD82 OE-LME (AAT2823 from Graz), which would collect the team on the 3rd. The fans arrived today on the following: Austrian Airlines Fokker 70 OE-LFP at 0953 (AAT2827 from Vienna) & MD83 OE-LMD at 1053 (AAT2855 from Graz), Lauda Air B.737-600 OE-LNK at 1050 (LDA5093 from Graz), Travel Services B.737-400 OK-TVR at 1434 (TVS116 from Prague) and Aer Lingus B.737-500 EI-CDF (EIN2202). Although well supported, it wasn't enough, as United were well into their European stride winning 2-1. This solidified their top position, and won the group over Marseille by three points.

23rd November 1999 - With only the briefest of breaks, United were back in European action. Today was the first match of the Second Group stage against Fiorentina in Pisa. The team travelled the previous day on Monarch Airlines B.757 G-MONK (MON9640), with the fans following the next day aboard Monarch A.300 G-MONS (MON9586). This proved to be a tough game for the Reds, and they were eventually beaten 2-0, their only defeat of the group.

8th December 1999 - Newcomers to the Champions League, Valencia, were United's opponents this evening. They arrived aboard SATA Boeing 737-300 CS-TGP (RZO9882 from Valencia) but there were no Spanish charters for the fans whatsoever, with the Irish arriving on Aer Lingus B.737-400 EI-BXA (EIN2216) & Ryanair B.737 EI-CNV (RYR5578). Interestingly, Corvette EC-DQG arrived the previous evening (from/to Valencia) and left immediately after the match. This aircraft was possibly carrying one of their players or the manager. United won the match comfortably 3-0, although the irony was that United would eventually win the group with Valencia finishing runners-up. The Spanish side would actually reach the Champions League final, only beaten by the side that knocked Manchester United out in the quarter-finals, Real Madrid!

9th December 1999 - Amazingly, having beaten Lokomotiv, Leeds were drawn to play another Russian team in the next round, Spartak Moscow. Although the team did not arrive through Manchester, Gromov Air Tupolev TU-134 RA-65926 wearing basic Aeroflot colours arrived during the evening to return the team and officials to Moscow.

1st March 2000 - After the winter break, European football returned with the visit of Bordeaux. Star Europe A.320 F-GRSG (SEU960L) was the transport for the team and officials. Football charters for the French fans were provided by a new French airline to Manchester, Aero Lyon. The airline operated charters with their recently acquired Douglas DC-10s. F-GLYS arrived at 1354 (AEY801 from Bordeaux) with the inbound passengers and F-BTDD at 2132 (AEY802) with the outbound passengers. Another charter was operated by Star Europe A.320 F-GRSI (SEU195L). The Irish arrived into Manchester on: Aer Lingus BAe.146s EI-CLJ (EIN2206) & EI-CSL (EIN2208), B.737-500 EI-CDG (EIN2202) and Ryanair B.737 EI-CKP (RYR5578). Finally, executive visitors arriving to watch United see off Bordeaux 2-0, were Learjets D-CDEN & N331SJ. The return match was played on the 7th March, and again Man United got the three points, winning 2-1.

15ᵗʰ March 2000 - Having been beaten by Fiorentina away earlier in the group, the return match at Old Trafford today was always going to be the toughest match of the group. The team arrived on the 14ᵗʰ aboard Volare A.320 EI-CUC (VLE1974/5 from/to Pisa), staying until the 16ᵗʰ. The Spanish fans arrived on Volare A.320 F-GJVX at 1129 (VLE1972 from Pisa) & Blue Panorama B.737-400 D-AHIS at 1310 (BPA5913 from Bologna). The Manchester United supporters club (Irish branch) were provided transport by Aer Lingus BAe.146s G-TBIC (EIN2208), EI-CLJ (EIN2204) & B.737-500 EI-CDG (EIN2202) and Ryanair B.737 EI-CKP (RYR5578). Learjet I-LIAD at 1500 (from Rome) was a first visit and other Learjets were G-OCFR & N331SJ, Citation 500 at 1510 OY-TKI (from Dublin) was also a first visit and finally regular BAe.125 EI-WDC at 1653 (from Dublin and returned after the match). The match itself virtually sealed United's passage into the next round, and Fiorentina's elimination with a 3-1 victory.

21ˢᵗ March 2000 - Man Utd finished the job by picking up a point at Valencia in the final group match, which meant they finished top by 3 points with Valencia as runners-up.

23ʳᵈ March 2000 - Leeds United were also making quiet advances towards the UEFA Cup Final. Their opponents this evening were Slavia Prague and CSA B.737-400 arrived at 0603 (CSA1666/7) to take a number of Leeds fans out to the game. Privatair B.737-700 HB-IIN arrived back at Manchester in the early hours of the 24ᵗʰ with the Leeds United team. The returning fans landed back later that evening aboard CSA B.737-400 OK-WGGG (CSA1666). Although they lost 2-1, they won the first leg at home 3-0 so qualified for the semi-finals, 4-2 on aggregate.

4ᵗʰ April 2000 - Man United's semi-final first leg against Real Madrid would be played away. For the first time they used Belgian airline Citybird to fly them out to Madrid. B.737-400 OO-CTW (CTB624) was the aircraft used which was also a first visit. Corsair B.737-400 F-GFUG (CRL374) was also used to take fans out to Madrid, with both aircraft returning the following day after United gained a valuable 0-0 draw. All they had to do now was beat Real Madrid at home in two weeks by one clear goal! Easy?

17ᵗʰ April 2000 - Iberia B.757 EC-FXV arrived at 1839 (IBE5058 from Madrid) on a flying visit, dropping off Real Madrid. This was also earmarked to take the team again on the 19ᵗʰ, but it went tech in Madrid, so B.757 EC-FYN (IBE5059 to Madrid) was used.

19ᵗʰ April - 2000 - What was surprising and possibly unprecedented for a Champion League quarter-final for a team like Real Madrid, was the absence of any additional fans' charters for the match. There were some lighter visitors however, with Mitsubishi MU-2 N973BB, BAe.125 G-OMGE and two Irish charters, Ryanair B.737s EI-CNT (RYR5574) & EI-COX (RYR5576). A fascinating but ultimately disappointing match saw the Spanish side go away from Old Trafford with a 3-2 victory, and knock United of the competition.

20ᵗʰ April 2000 - The final football-related flight of the season was again connected with Leeds United, which also proved to be their season swansong. Having lost 2-0 in Turkey two weeks earlier, Leeds had a mountain to climb against Galatasaray, which proved just too much. The final score in the second-leg at Elland Road was 2-2 which meant Galatasaray would be in the UEFA Cup Final where they would meet Arsenal. On the 21ˢᵗ, THY B.737-400 arrived at 0034 (THY3753/4) to take the Turkish side home.

14th September 1999 – Croatian Airlines A.319 9A-CTH is seen having recently arrived with Croatia Zagreb FC. Formed in 1989 after the break-up of Yugoslavia, Croatian Airlines began operations with a single Cessna 402. Two years later they signed an agreement with Adria Airways, allowing them to lease an MD82 to commence jet services between Zagreb-Split. However, due to the Croatian War of Independence and closure of the airspace over Croatia, they were forced to suspend operations. In 1992 as soon as flights restarted, Croatia Airlines acquired three B.737s from Lufthansa and in the same year they opened their first international route to Frankfurt. (Denis Norman)

15th September 1999 – Croatian Airlines received their first Airbus A.320, 9A-CTF 'Rijeka' in 1997, and their first Airbus A.319, 9A-CTG 'Zadar' seen here in 1998. By 1999 two were A.319 9A-CTI & A.320 9A-CTJ, and they started disposing of their Boeing 737 fleet. They have been regularly serving Manchester since 1993, with weekly summer charters to Pula and Split, carrying well over 1 million passengers annually from 2000. In July 2009, they carried their 20,000,000th passenger! (Denis Norman)

28th September 1999 – This was the first visit to Manchester by French airline Aeris, although they were only a re-incarnation of Air Toulouse. Boeing 737-300 F-GNFC was purchased from Viva Air in July this year, and was operated until November 2003 when the airline ceased trading. (Terry Shone)

28th September 1999 – Having recently arrived from Marseille, is Corsair B.747-300 F-GSEA, seen basking in the autumn sunshine amongst the Airbuses of Air 2000 and Swissair. (Mark White)

1st November 1999 – OE-LME was one two Austrian Airlines MD80s seen at Manchester over the next couple of days. This aircraft brought in Sturm Graz, and is seen shortly after arrival. It operated with the airline until 2005, when they phased out their few remaining MD80s. (Nik French)

2nd November 1999 – Lauda Air B.737-600 OE-LNK is seen making its first visit to Manchester. The airline had disposed of its entire Boeing 737 fleet, comprising of both the -600 & -800 models by 2013. This aircraft operated the final Lauda Air B.737 flight on 2nd April 2013. (Nik French)

2nd November 1999 – The Austrian football fans seem to give excellent 'away support' to their sides playing in Europe. The visit of Sturm Graz to Manchester provided several football charters. Austrian Airlines MD80 OE-LMD seen here on short finals, also flew the final Austrian Airlines MD80 flight on 22nd June 2005. (Denis Norman)

8th December 1999 – CS-TGP was one of five Boeing 737s operated by the Portuguese airline from 1995-2004. Established in December 1990, SATA International operates scheduled flights between the Madeira Islands, mainland Portugal and other destinations in Europe and North America, as well as charter flights. From 2008-2011, they also intermittently operated scheduled flights between Manchester and Funchal with Airbus A.320s. (Terry Shone)

1st March 2000 – Aerolyon was a long haul airline based at Lyon, flying from various French airports including Lyon, Paris, Brest, Nantes and Bordeaux to the Caribbean, West Indies and other overseas French territories. Owned by French travel company Nouvelles Frontieres, who also owned Corsair. In 1996, Aerolyon purchased their first DC-10, F-BTDD (above), and a second purchased two years later was F-GLYS (below). A third added in 2002 was F-GTDF, but the airline would not expand any further as they went into liquidation the same year. (Above Nik French, below Denis Norman)

1st March – The latest Star Europe Airbus A.320 to visit Manchester was F-GRSG. It had arrived yesterday with the Bordeaux team and officials, and stayed until the 2nd March. This aircraft was sold to Eurofly in November 2004 as I-EEZH. (Nik French)

SEASON 2000/2001
Manchester United UEFA Champions League
Leeds United UEFA Champions League
FA Cup Semi-Final (Arsenal v Spurs)
Liverpool UEFA Cup

The 2000/01 season was Manchester United's ninth in the Premier League, and their twenty-sixth consecutive season in the top division of English football. United won the Premier League for the third successive season, and the seventh time since its inauguration in 1993. They were less successful in cup competitions, going out in the fourth round of the FA Cup, the fourth round of the League Cup and the quarter-finals of the Champions League.

9th August 2000 – The football charters began early this season. Leeds United had to play a two-legged qualifying match against 1860 Munich. The first leg was played today at Elland Road, which Leeds won 2-1. Balair B.767 HB-IHU arrived at 2305 (BBB322/3) to fly the German fans home. However, its departure was delayed until 0252 on the 10th due to a night-time curfew at Munich. The return match two weeks later was again won by Leeds, 1-0, which meant they had fully qualified for the UEFA Champions League. Leeds United would eventually go all the way to the semi-finals, only to be beaten by Valencia.

13th September 2000 - Having won the Premier League yet again, Manchester United went straight into the group stages of the Champions League, unlike Leeds. Their first match in the group was against Belgian champions, Anderlecht. The team arrived on the 12th aboard Sobelair B.737-400 OO-VEJ (SLR4391), which later positioned out to Luxembourg. Match day attracted just one football charter and a second Sobelair flight, again operated by B.737-400 OO-VEJ (SLR4395), which left after dropping off the fans. Two executive visitors were BAe.125 CS-DNL and Beech 200 PH-ATM (TLP9B) both from Brussels, and after Anderlecht had been thoroughly beaten 5-1, Sobelair B.737-300 OO-SLK arrived to take the fans home. B.737-400 OO-VEJ came in yet again to collect the team.

19th September 2000 - European Airlines B.737 G-CEAE (EAF2124) was Manchester United's transport to Kiev for their next match with Dynamo Kiev. Another European aircraft, BAC 1-11 G-AYOP (EAF8408), took the fans out to witness United earn a valuable away point from a goalless draw.

26th September 2000 - Another away match and signs that maybe the wheels were coming off the bandwagon! Their opponents today were PSV Eindhoven, who inflicted a rare group match defeat on Manchester United, losing 3-1. The team again used European Airlines for their flight to Eindhoven, BAC 1-11 G-AYOP (EAF8408).

18th October 2000 – Manchester United got their revenge on PSV Eindhoven tonight with a 3-1 victory. The Dutch side arrived at 1341 the day before aboard Sobelair B.737-400 OO-VEJ (SLR4415 from Eindhoven), leaving later for Brussels. Transavia B.757 PH-TKD (TRA8297 from Eindhoven) was the only fans' charter, but there were two interesting executive visitors: Sabreliner N265SP (from/to Luton) and Martinair Citation 650 PH-MFX (MPH3151), which dropped off a number of passengers that were picked up again the following day on another Martinair Citation 650, this time PH-MEX. The team were also picked up on the 19th, travelling home aboard Sobelair B.737-400 OO-SBJ (SLR1416).

24th October 2000 - Anderlecht were proving the surprise team of the group, further solidifying this label tonight by beating Manchester United 2-1, their second defeat in the group. The Reds travelled out to Brussels the day before, again using European Airlines. B.737-200 G-CEAD (EAF2126) which departed at 1027, and returned in the early hours of the 25th.

8th November 2000 – The final group match was a rather nerve racking affair! Only a victory for Manchester United would guarantee their qualification into the second Group stage, which they managed - only just! Their opponents, Dynamo Kiev, arrived on the 7th and brought another new airline to Manchester, Aerosvit, aboard B.737-700 UR-VVA (AEV557 from Kiev). Not surprisingly, there were no extra fans charters and UR-VVA turned up again after the match for the Dynamo Kiev team. United just edged it 1-0, but finished second in the group, two points behind Anderlecht.

21st November 2000 – Greek side Panathinaikos, a new team to Manchester United, were the first opponents in the second group stage. Macedonian Airlines B.737-300 SX-BMC (MCS2775) was the team's chariot, arriving the day before and staying until the 22nd. The team was also well supported, with three football charters arriving on the match day: Galaxy Airlines B.737-400s at 1136 (GAL7000 from Athens) & SX-BFP at 1329 (GAL7020 from Athens) and Cronus Airlines B.737-300 SX-BBT at 1225 (CUS4592 from Athens). Both airlines were making their first visits to Manchester. However, the fans enthusiasm for travelling to Manchester was not matched by their team's spirit on the pitch, losing 3-1. On the 6th December, Manchester United travelled to Austria where they comfortably beat Sturm Graz 2-0. Macedonian B.737-300 SX-BMC turned up again on the 7th December, bringing the Olympiakos team to play Liverpool in the UEFA Cup at Anfield.

14th February 2001 – Manchester United remained unbeaten in the group when they travelled to Valencia, where they battled out a 0-0 draw. They would face Valencia again the following week, when the Spanish side travelled to Old Trafford.

20th February 2001 – Entering the Champions League for the first time last year and making it all the way to the final, Valencia were still proving a tough team to beat. They would face United again tonight, and make things as difficult as possible for them. The end result was a 1-1 draw, but qualification was looking good for both teams. Valencia arrived at 2119 on the 18th on a strange choice of aircraft, Islandflug B.737-300 TF-FDA (HHH2070), leaving an hour later for Paris-CDG. There was just one football charter on match day, Futura B.737-400 EC-GNZ at 1031 (FUA7961 from Valencia). Executive visitors were BAe.125 EI-WJN, Citation 550 EI-DAB & MU-2 N973BB.

7th March 2001 – Maybe Valencia officials had a word with the top brass at United, saying what a nice aircraft the Reds had flown out to Athens on, namely Islandflug

B.737-300 TF-FDA! The whipping boys of the group were a little more robust on this occasion, holding United to a 1-1 draw.

13th March 2001 – The final match of the group saw Manchester United playing host to the extremely well supported Sturm Graz. The result would be fairly academic as Manchester United, along with Valencia, had already qualified for the knockout stages. It would be decided by the end of the evening who would finish in the all important top spot, Manchester United or Valencia. Hamburg International B.737-700 D-ASKH (HHI8762 from Graz) brought the team in on the 12th, and there were football charters aplenty on match day with Lauda Air B.737-400 OE-LNH at 0814 (LDA429 from Graz), Austrian Airlines MD80s OE-LMD at 1040 (AUA2815 from Graz), OE-LMA at 1102 (AUA2817), Eurowings A.319 D-AKNF at 0944 (EWG5178 from Graz) and the real surprise was Lauda Air B.777 OE-LPB at 1013 (LDA423). Executive visitors included Citation 501 OE-FDM, Citation 525 OE-FLG- and Agusta 109 EI-MEL. After United's comfortable 3-0 victory and with Valencia recording a win, both teams finished the group on 12 points, but Valencia would top the group with a better goal difference. Manchester United would now face the mighty Bayern Munich in the quarter finals.

3rd April 2001 – Another nerve wracking Champions League quarter-final was to take place over the two legs, the first of which would take place today. In preparation for this, Bayern Munich arrived on the 2nd aboard Aero Lloyd Airbus A.321 D-ALAP (AEF9910 from Munich), staying until the 4th. Today's football charters were Eurowings A.319 D-AKNG at 1022 (EWG5198 from Dusseldorf) and a further three Aero Lloyd flights with Airbus A.320 D-ALAE at 1033 (AEF992 from Frankfurt), MD-83 D-ALLF at 1108 (AEF9920 from Munich) & Airbus A.321 D-ALAI at 1144 (AEF9924 from Munich) and also Learjet 55 D-CVIP at 1354 (WDL055 from Frankfurt). Irish support for United consisted of Aer Lingus B.737-400 EI-BXD (EIN2206/7), BAe.125s EI-WDC & EI-WJN and Citation 550 EI-PAL. The signs were not good for the return leg for United, losing 1-0 against an efficiently organised Bayern Munich and an even tougher game to face in Germany in two weeks time.

8th April 2001 – In between Champion League games, today Old Trafford played host to a battle of North London clubs in the FA Cup semi-final. This produced plenty of extra traffic, starting with the airlines: Maersk CRJ G-MSKT (MSK094/5 from/to Luton), Monarch Airlines B.757 G-MONK (MON9532/3 from/to Luton), European BAC 1-11s G-AYOP EAF8546/7 from/to Stansted) & G-AZMF (EAF8548/9 from/to Stansted), British World ATP G-OBWR (BWL3406/7 from/to Stansted) & B.737-300 G-OBWX (BWL5243/4 from/to Stansted), PLM Jetstream 31 G-PLAJ (PLM881 from Luton), British Airways upgraded a couple of their Shuttle flights using Boeing 767-300s G-BNWZ & G-BZHB and also some extra B.757 flights with G-BIKC (BAW528/9 from/to Heathrow), G-BIKW (BAW9209/10 from/to Stansted) & G-CPEL (BAW526/7 from/to Heathrow) and also B.747 G-BDXG (BAW091C from/to Stansted). British Midland laid on a couple of extra A.321 flights with G-MIDC (BMA8919/20 from/to Luton) & G-MIDH (BMA2582/3 from/to Heathrow). Executive visitors were BAe.125s G-IFTE, G-OLDD, G-OMGD & G-WBPR; Citation 550s G-FJET, G-SPUR & N145DF; Learjet 45 G-JRJR (GDΛ088B from Luton) and Cessna 421 N202AA (from/to Elstree)

18th April 2001 - Manchester United had a mountain climb to try and overturn Bayern Munich's advantage after the first leg. The team flew out to Munich again aboard Islandflug B.737-300 TF-FDA (HHH2104), but flew home in the early hours of the 19th having endured a further defeat, 2-1, and exit from the competition.

16th May 2001 – The final football charters of this season took place today, in connection with the UEFA Cup final taking place in Dortmund between Liverpool and Deportivo Alaves. The sheer amount of fans travelling out to Dortmund meant that Liverpool airport could not cope, so the following flights left from Manchester and all returned the following morning: Air Liberte DC-10 F-GLMX (TAT8049), Aero Lloyd A.321 D-ALAL (AEF9958), Sterling B.737-800 OY-SEI (SNB1207) which were all first visits and also Corsair B.747 F-GLNA (CRL816).

1st August 2000 – Pulkovo Aviation Tupolev TU-134 RA-65113 brought Zenit St. Petersburg to Manchester for a UEFA Intertoto Cup match the following evening with Bradford City. The pedigree of the Russian side proved far too strong for Bradford, winning 3-0 on the night and 4-0 on aggregate. Pulkovo Aviation merged with Rossiya Aviation in 2006, and RA-65113 was withdrawn in April 2008. (Terry Shone)

12ᵗʰ September 2000 – Sobelair B.737-400 OO-VEJ was the transport for Anderlecht FC for their match with Manchester United. The airline, formed in 1946, operated mostly non-scheduled passenger and cargo flights in its fifty-eight year history. As far back as 1949, it was 72% owned by Sabena and for the only time in its existence, it operated scheduled flights to the Democratic Republic of Congo during the 1950s. They entered the jet age in 1971, when a second-hand SE.210 Caravelle was acquired from Sabena. Over the next twenty-five years, they operated a couple of B.707s, a fleet of Boeing 737s and a two B.767-300s. Their downfall however came in 2001 with the demise of Swissair, and later Sabena. Although Sobelair was purchased by a group of investors, it was declared bankrupt in January 2004. (Denis Norman)

18ᵗʰ October 2000 – PH-TKD was the last of Transavia's four Boeing 757s to visit Manchester, arriving with Eindhoven fans. (Nik French)

7th November 2000 – Aerosvit B.737-300 UR-VVA was making the airline's only visit to Manchester today. Established in 1994, the Ukrainian airline built up a sizeable route network and fleet over the next twenty years. They ceased trading in April 2013, with some aircraft being transferred to Ukraine International. (Denis Norman)

21st November 2000 – Galaxy Airlines were short-lived Greek operators, trading briefly from 1999-2001. Two of their aircraft, B.737-400 SX-BFV (above) and B.737-300 SX-BFP (overleaf) were carrying Panathinaikos fans. During 2000, the airline had a summer programme of flights from Manchester to a variety of Greek destinations. (Nik French)

21st November 2000 – B.737-300 SX-BFP (Denis Norman)

20th February 2001 – Islandflug B.737-300 TF-FDA, wearing Sunbird titles, brought Valencia FC to Manchester. It was then used by Manchester United as their personal transport for the next few away games. It became a regular visitor during 2001, operating a summer programme to various European destinations until its last visit on 15th October 2001. In January 2002, it was sold to Pluna as CX-PUA. (Nik French)

12th March 2001 – Lauda Air B.777 OE-LPB was a most welcome first visit today, arriving with Sturm Graz fans. Fourteen years later this aircraft is still in service, now one of five B.777s operated by Austrian Airlines since Lauda Air ceased trading in April 2013. (Nik French)

12th March 2001 – Formed two years previously, Hamburg International was another new airline to Manchester. B.737-700 D-ASKH was used today to bring in Sturm Graz for their Champions League match with Man U. This aircraft later became D-AHIA and served the German airline until they went bankrupt in October 2010. (Allan Jones)

13th March 2001 – OE-LMA was the last Austrian Airlines MD80 to visit Manchester. Along with the others it was disposed of during 2004 and sold to Nordic Airlink as SE-RDT, operating with them for a further three years. (Denis Norman)

2nd April 2001 – Airbus A.321 D-ALAP was the first of four Aero Lloyd aircraft to visit in connection with the Bayern Munich-Manchester United match taking place the following evening, bringing in the German team. (Allan Jones)

3rd April 2001 – Following on from the visit of A.319 D-AKNF in March, today D-AKNG became the second Eurowings jet to Manchester. The airline would make one further appearance in their own right on 24th April 2002, as in December 2006 Lufthansa took a 49% share of the airline and became part of the Lufthansa group. (Nik French)

3rd April 2001 – Aero Lloyd Airbus A.320 D-ALAE operated for the airline until their demise in 2003. After a couple of years with Niki, it's been operating for Airbus as a 'Fuel Cell' demonstration aircraft since 2006. (Denis Norman)

3rd April 2001 – Seen here on short finals is Aero Lloyd Airbus A.321 D-ALAI, sporting a special livery. The aircraft is promoting Trigema, a German sports and leisure wear manufacturer. (Denis Norman)

3rd April 2001 – During 2001, Aero Lloyd would phase out their remaining MD80s from their fleet, so today's visit of D-ALLF would prove to be the final one to visit Manchester. In fact D-ALLF would operate the very final Aero Lloyd MD80 service on the 6th November 2001. (Denis Norman)

3rd April 2001 – Surprisingly for a quarter-final, there were few executive visitors for the Bayern Munich-Manchester United match. The visit today of Learjet 55 D-CVIP seen here, was the only German executive visitor. This was in sharp contrast to the later years, when there would be many more arrivals for match days! (Denis Norman)

SEASON 2001/2002
Manchester United UEFA Champions League
England World Cup

The 2001–2002 season was Manchester United's tenth in the Premier League and their twenty-seventh consecutive season in the top division of English football. This season would prove to be rather dismal compared the previous three years. The club finished in third place in the Premier League, their lowest finish in its short history, and they were knocked out of the FA Cup in the fourth round. League Cup success was not expected, and the club duly obliged by playing what was effectively a reserve team against a strong Arsenal side in the third round. United's best success in the 2001–2002 season came in the UEFA Champions League, in which they reached the semi-finals before being knocked out by Bayer Leverkusen on away goals. Ultimately, United's failure to win anything boiled down a dismal run of form in November and early December when they suffered five defeats in seven league games, including three defeats in a row during December. They also lost six home games in the Premier League, their worst home record since the 1977–1978 season. They only lost three more league games all season, but that terrible form earlier in the campaign counted against United for the rest of the season when they finished ten points behind champions Arsenal (who sealed their crown by beating United 1–0 at Old Trafford in the penultimate game of the season) and three points behind runners-up Liverpool.

12th August 2001 – KLM Excel made their first appearance at Manchester with EMB-145 PH-RXB (AXL828/9 t/f Cardiff), taking fans to Cardiff for the FA Charity Shield.

1st September 2001 – Electra Douglas DC-10 SX-CVH took a plane load of England fans out to Munich for the England-Germany qualifying match, one which finally saw England as the dominant force, winning 5-1.

11th September 2001 – Manchester United travelled out today to Athens, for what was to be their first group match of the Champions League. The game however, was later cancelled due to the events in America. Manchester United flew back home the following morning, and the game was re-scheduled for the 10th October.

18th September 2001 – Lille FC arrived in Manchester aboard VLM Fokker 50 OO-VLO (VLM801) for their game on the 19th with Man United. This aircraft positioned later for Rotterdam, while another Fokker 50, OO-VLS, positioned after the match to return the team to Lille. It also produced two charters on match day, EMB-110 LX-SKS at 1002 (SKS112 from Lille) & Euralair B.737-800 F-GRNB at 1359 (EUL2216 from Lille). A closely fought contest saw United do just enough to record a 1-0 victory.

25th September 2001 – United played Deportivo La Coruna today in Santiago, losing 2-1. The team flew out the previous day on Channel Express B.737-300 TF-ELR (EXS5005), while the fans flew out on European B.737 G-CEAF (EAF2367) & Cougar Airways Boeing 727 G-OPMN (GCR112), all returning in the early hours of the 26th.

6th October 2001 – While the old Wembley was being demolished for a new stadium, England began to play their matches around the country and were in the middle of trying to qualify for the 2002 World Cup Finals. Old Trafford was the venue for one such match today against Greece. The Greeks arrived on the 4th October aboard Fischer Air B.737-300 OK-FUN at 1216 (FFR4933 from Athens). Aircraft connected with today's match were Cessna 414 N414FZ, Citation 550s G-FCDB & G-SPUR, BAe.125 G-HCFR and Gulfstream 4 N18WF (from Amsterdam). A second Fischer Air B.737-300, OK-FIT, arrived at 1911 (FFR/933) to take the defeated Greek team back to Athens.

10th October 2001 – Presumably there was no Channel Express B.737 available, so Manchester United chartered Maersk B.737-700 OY-MRG (DAN1533) to take them out to Athens. This was the re-arranged match against Olympiakos from last month, which this time United won comfortably 2-0.

17th October 2001 – One of most exciting teams in the 2001- 2002 Champions League were Spanish side Deportivo La Coruna, which just happened to be in United's group! The Spaniards gave United a lesson in finishing which left the fans stunned. Deportivo Le Coruna won the game 3-2, but both Deportivo and United were beginning to look like they would be the ones progressing to the next phase. Futura B.737-400 EC-GUG (FUA7631 from La Coruna) arrived the day before with Deportivo, staying until the 18th. The only extra visitors for match day were Irish related, with Aer Lingus B.737-500 EI-CDA (EIN2216/7) and BAe.125s EI-RRR & EI-WJN.

23rd October 2001 – The second European home in seven days saw the return visit of Olympiakos. The team arrived on the 22nd aboard Axon Airlines B.737-300 SX-BLM at 1125 (AX9315 from Athens) 3-0. The following day three fans charters were another Axon Airlines B.737, -700 SX-BLU at 1510 (AXO9513) and two Cronus Airlines B.737-400s - SX-BGH at 1211 (CUS4602) & SX-BGJ at 1230 (CUS4604). Citation 550 OE-GIL, which arrived at 1300 was also football-related. A third Axon Airlines B.737, -400 SX-BLM, arrived at 2301 to take the Greeks home after a 2-0 defeat.

31st October 2001 – Manchester United's final match of the group took place today against Lille. Channel Express B.737-300 TF-ELP was used once again to fly the team out. The game ended 1-1, which left both United and Deportivo both at the top of the group on 10pts, although the Spanish team had the better goal difference.

20th November 2001 - Bayern Munich were the tough nut to crack in the second group stage. Facing the Germans away in the first leg, United earned a credible 1-1 draw.

5th December 2001 – For today's latest match, Portuguese side Boavista were new to Manchester United, but they were fairly easy opposition for the Reds, easily winning 3-0. The team arrived on the 3rd aboard SATA International B.737-300 CS-TGQ (RZO9550/1 from/to Oporto). The game did not inspire any fans charters, with the only additional traffic being BAe.125 EI-WJN & Mitsubishi MU-2 N973BB.

20th February 2002 - Manchester United got their European ambitions under way again, with an away match against Nantes, which ended 1-1.

26th February 2002 – The return match with Nantes was considerably more one sided that the away match the previous week, with United chalking up another easy win, 5-1. Nantes arrived on the 25th aboard Aeris B.737-300 F-GNFC at 1111 (AIS376/7 from/to Nantes), departing on the 27th. This match generated much interest with the French, and the following charters arrived during match day: Star Europe A.320s F-GRSD (SEU910L), F-GRSG (SEU912L) & F-GRSH (SEU908L); Euralair B.737-800 at 0955

(EUL296) and Aigle Azur B.737-200 F-GMJD at 1008 (AAF9251). Lighter visitors were PA-31 EI-CNM, BAe.125 EI-WDC and Learjet 45 G-OLDJ.

13th March 2002 - Bayern Munich arrived the previous day on Aero Lloyd A.321 D-ALAM (AEF9920 from Munich), which positioned later in the afternoon to Hessenthal. Surprisingly, the only two football charters on match day were Condor B.757-300 D-ABOH at 1159 (CFG9134) & Aer Lingus B.737-500 EI-CDF (EIN2218/9). However, there was a little more private interest with executive visitors Citation 550s D-IAWA & OY-BZT; Citation 560 D-CAUW, Gulf 5 EI-CVT, Mitsubishi MU-2 N973BB, Agusta 109 EI-MEL, BAe.125 EI-WJN, Learjet G-OLDC and Flandre Air Beech 1900 F-GLNF. On the 14th March, Aero Lloyd A.321 D-ALAP (AEF9920P/9921) arrived to take Bayern Munich home, with both teams relatively satisfied after a goalless draw, which virtually guaranteed their progress into the quarter-finals.

19th March 2002 – Manchester United finished the job today by beating Boavista 3-0 away from home. Bayern Munich and Man Utd now both topped the group with 12pts, but this time Manchester United had the advantage with a superior goal difference.

2nd April 2002 – The team that were looking like contenders for the final were Deportivo La Coruna, drawn to play Manchester United in the quarter finals. The first leg was played in Spain, and Manchester United pulled off a sensational 2-0 victory, giving them a solid base to defend, if necessary, for the return leg at Old Trafford the following week.

10th April 2002 – There were slip-ups, as Man United defended their two goal first leg advantage over Deportivo La Coruna, winning this leg 3-2. The Spanish team arrived on the 9th aboard Futura B.737-400 EC-GUG at 1210 (FUA7641 from La Coruna), leaving on the 11th. There were no fans charters from Deportivo, but two that were United related were Aer Lingus A.320 EI-CVD (EIN2216/7) & Maersk B.737-700 OY-MRK at 1902 (DA1901 from Copenhagen), along with Citation 550 EI-PAL, Citation 560 CS-DNY, Beech 200 F-GHCS, Learjet 60 OY-LJM and Mitsubishi MU-2 N973BB.

24th April 2002 – Manchester United had home advantage for their semi-final first leg match with Bayer Leverkusen. The German team name derives from 'Bayer' the German pharmaceutical company and 'Leverkusen' is the town where their HQ is situated. They arrived on the 23rd aboard Condor B.767-300 D-ABUC at 1125 (CFG144/5 from/to Cologne), departing after the match. There were plenty of charters and executive visitors for this one, with Aero Lloyd A.320 D-ALAJ at 1527 (AEF9920 from Dusseldorf) & A.321 D-ALAO at 0948 (AEF9930 from Dusseldorf); LTU A.330-300 at 0951 (LTU3000 from Dusseldorf), Eurowings A.319 D-AKNG at 1522 (EWG5338 from Dusseldorf) with German fans, and Aer Lingus A.320 EI-CVB (EIN2208/9) & A.321 EI-CPC (EIN2216/7) with the Irish United followers. Finally there were plenty of German biz-jets, with Learjet 35 D-COKE, Learjet 55 D-CVIP, Hawker 800 D-Chef, Citation 525 D-IHAP and PA-46 D-EEJF. The game itself went in the Germans favour, earning a 2-2 draw and two valuable away goals.

30th April 2002 – The Manchester United bandwagon ended tonight, when they could only manage a 1-1 draw, 3-3 on aggregate but going out on away goals. This was despite travelling in their largest 'bus' to date, British Airways B.767-300 G-BZHC, returning in the early hours of the 1st May.

12th September 2001 – Channel Express B.737-300 TF-ELP is seen arriving back at Manchester after an aborted attempt for United to kick-off their latest Champions League campaign. Between 2001 and 2002, the airline temporarily became the airline of choice for the transportation of the Reds across Europe. (Allan Jones)

18th September 2001 – Initially leased to the short lived British North West Airlines, EMB-110 LX-SKS was operated by Belgian air taxi operator, Skyservice until November 2002. It now operates Ghana. (Geoff Ball)

24th September 2001 – When Libra Holidays became the majority shareholder of Sabre Airways in November 2000, the airline would eventually be re-branded as Excel Airways. In 2001, a former Sabre Airways Chief Executive purchased three Boeing 727s as part of that sale. The three Boeing 727-200s, G-BPND, G-OKJN & G-OPMN operated for newly formed Cougar until 2003 when it folded. G-OPMN seen here, was the only passenger aircraft in the fleet, the other two were operated as pure-cargo aircraft. (Denis Norman)

23rd October 2001 – Both airlines involved in the transportation of Olympiakos fans for their match with Manchester United would have ceased operating by the end of the year.

Axon Airlines B.737-700 SX-BLU made several visits to Manchester between 2000 and 2001 with three different aircraft. The independent airline launched in 1999, also operated scheduled services to Brussels, Milan and Paris. However, they would be one of three Greek airlines that would have ceased trading by the end of 2001, mainly due to the public's lack of confidence in flying after the events of 9/11. At the time, Axon Airlines were also planning to purchase the country's struggling national flag carrier, Olympic Airways, which was surprising considering the airline had been losing money since the day it started. (Nik French)

23rd October 2001 – Cronus Airlines B.737-400 SX-BGJ is seen here after its recent arrival at Manchester with Olympiakos fans. Cronus was the third and final Greek airline that ceased trading by the end of 2001, although for slightly different reasons to those of Galaxy and Axon. Established in 1994 by a Greek construction entrepreneur, operations began the following year with a single aircraft flying expats between Greece and Germany. They also operated charter flights to various tourist destinations. In 1997, they expanded and by adding two more Boeing 737 aircraft to their fleet, and gradually became the largest privately owned airline on Greece. In Spring 2001, a code-share agreement was signed with Aegean Airlines, and the airline's aircraft were painted in Aegean colours with Aegean-Cronus titles. In October 2001 Cronus was fully acquired by Aegean. (Nik French)

24th October 2001 – Visiting in connection with the Manchester United-Olympiakos match, Citation 550 OE-GIL which was originally built in 1979, made its first visit. In 2015, it is still current on the Austrian register. (Denis Norman)

3rd December 2001 – CS-TGQ seen here was one of three SATA International B.737-300s to visit between 1996 and 2001. Operating five Boeing 737s in total all had been replaced by Airbus A.310/A.320 aircraft by 2004. (Lee Collins)

25th February 2002 – Although Aeris B.737-300 F-GNFU made its first visit today, it first appeared as an airframe in 1991 for Monarch Airlines (G-MONM). After Monarch, it visited again as an Air Europa machine, under four different registrations! When Aeris ceased trading in November 2003, it was sold to Slovak Airlines. (Nik French)

26th February 2002 – Parked on T2 with three other football related flights is Euralair B.737-800 F–GRNE on its first visit, along with Star Europe A.320s F-GRSD/GRSG & GRSH, plus Air France A.320 F-GLGH. Having been existence since 1964, Euralair filed for bankruptcy protection in November 2003, but was saved from liquidation by a last-minute takeover. In February 2004, they restarted as Air Horizons with a much reduced fleet, but by November 2005 they had finally ceased trading. (Nik French)

26th February 2002 – This Boeing 737-200 classic, F-GMJD, operated by a new airline to Manchester, Aigle Azur, brought in yet more Nantes fans. In 2015 the airline is still trading, but this aircraft was sold later in 2002 to Bali Air as PK-KJN. (Denis Norman)

13th March 2002 – Condor B.757-300 D-ABOH is seen making the first visit of one of their 'extended' Boeing 757s. This aircraft and airline are still very much in existence in 2015. (Denis Norman)

24th April 2002 – Citation 550 EI-PAL was a fairly regular visitor to Manchester between 2000 and 2003, particularly when Manchester United were playing a home match! In 2004 it was re-registered as G-IPAL. (Denis Norman)

24th April 2002 – The visit of Bayer Leverkusen produced numerous football charters, the largest of these being the first visit of LTU Airbus A.330-300 D-AERF. With an operating history dating back to 1956, this successful German airline was taken over in 2007 by Air Berlin. It was announced the following year that the trademark 'LTU' would no longer be used. The last flight under an LTU call sign was the 13th October 2009 on a flight from Montreal to Dusseldorf, and was fully dissolved into Air Berlin thereafter. (Nik French)

24th April 2002 – Further flights in connection with this match were Aero Lloyd A.321 D-ALAO & A.320 D-ALAJ, with the latter aircraft making its first visit. Following the airline's collapse in late 2003, D-ALAO was sold to Spirit Airlines as N584NK, and D-ALAJ ended up with Volare as I-PEKU. (Above Nik French, below Denis Norman)

SEASON 2002/2003
Manchester United UEFA Champions League/Premiership
Blackburn Rovers UEFA Cup
England World Cup

The 2002–2003 season was Manchester United's eleventh season in the Premier League and their twenty-eighth consecutive season in the top division of English football. This season saw the club finish at the top of the Premier League table, after their lowest finish in the history of the Premier League the previous season, when they came third. In order to win the title, the team had to pull Arsenal back from an eight-point lead at the beginning of March, winning the title by five points. Manchester United also finished as runners-up in the League Cup, with Liverpool eventually taking the prize. They were knocked out of the FA Cup in the fifth round by Arsenal, and fell short in the Champions League, exiting at the quarter finals after an amazing encounter with Real Madrid in the second leg.

The highlight of the season was undoubtedly Old Trafford playing host to the UEFA Champion League final on the 28th May 2003. So it was just as well that Manchester United and the other competing English teams, didn't make it!

August started with two football friendlies which involved local teams. Manchester City travelled to Hamburg aboard New Air Fokker 50 OY-MMS (2nd), while Verona arrived at Manchester (8th) for a pre-season friendly with Bolton Wanderers, using Farnair Europe Fokker F.27 HB-ILJ.

14th August 2002 - Due to their poor showing last season, Manchester United would have to go through a qualifying round before they could join the competition at the group stage. This would be a two-legged game against Hungarian side Zalaegerszeg with the first game being played today in Hungary. United travelled to Budapest on the 13th aboard MD-83 TF-MDE (MDI8122). Futura B.737-400 (FUA5730) was chartered for the fans on match day. United lost 1-0, which could have been the reason for the enthusiastic turnout for the second leg.

27th August 2002 – The Hungarians chartered Icelandair Holidays B.757 TF-FIW (ICE854 from Budapest via Graz) and must have sensed a major upset after doing so well in the first leg. The support for this qualifying match was very impressive, with a pair of Bulgarian Air Charter TU-154s, LZ-LCA at 1251 (VSR4377 from Samellek) & LZ-LCS at 1227 (VKS4375 from Samellek); Malev Fokker 70 HA-LME at 1325 (MAH2666 from Budapest) & B.737-400 HA-LEU at 1445 (MAH1444 from Budapest); and Prime Airbus A.300 G-HLAD at 1335 (HLA966 from Budapest). With all that support, you would expect Zalaegerszeg to do better – but they were thrashed 5-1!

18th September 2002 – The real hard work would now start, beginning with a new team to face Manchester United, in the form of Israeli side Maccabi Haifa. However, they proved inferior opposition again, with United winning easily 5-2. The team arrived the previous day aboard EL AL/Israir Boeing 757 4X-EBM (ISR105), which returned to collect them on the 20th. There was also a fans' charter on the 17th, with Freebird MD-80 TC-FBT (FHY112 from Istanbul, and the airline making its first visit to Manchester. Maccabi was another well supported team, with the following charters on match day: EL

AL B.737-800 4X-EKI at 1157 (ELY5061), B.757s 4X-EBM (again) at 1509 (ISR105) & 4X-EBT at 1256 (ELY5067); and another airline first visit with the arrival of Bosphorus European A.300 at 1303 (BHY081 from Istanbul).

20th September 2002 – Blackburn Rovers were briefly, competing in this year's UEFA Cup. Today they had first round two-legged match with CSKA Sofia. The team arrived on the third Bulgaria Air Charter TU-154 to visit this year, LZ-LCI at 1110 (BUC381). The fans were aboard Travel Services B.737-800 OK-TVQ (TVS020 from Prague). The game ended 1-1, but Blackburn got a 3-3 draw away from home two weeks later, travelling out on British Midland A.330 G-WWBD (BMA7971 to Sofia), which put them through on away goals. However, they would be knocked out in Round two against Celtic.

24th September 2002 – Two wins out of two when United travelled to Germany to play Bayer Leverkusen, pulling off a 2-1 away win. The team left on the 23rd aboard British Midland A.321 G-MIDA (BMA7955), with the fans travelling on Air 2000 B.757 G-OOBA (AMM5548), both to Cologne.

1st October 2002 – The Greek side Olympiakos had again the misfortune of being drawn into the same group as Manchester United, and the outcome was the same - a Manchester United victory, 4-0. With the disappearance of Galaxy, Cronus and Axon, there weren't many airlines for the team to use, so Aegean made its first appearance at Manchester on the 30th September when B.737-400 SX-BLM arrived at 1222 (AEE4200 from Athens) on its first visit, along with a fans' charter operated by Islandflug B.737-400 TF-ELV at 1429 (HHI4255 from Athens). Match day provided Macedonian B.737-400 SX-BMA at 1138 (MCS2775), another Aegean B.737-400, SX-BGR, at 1333 (AEE4800) and Hola Airlines B.737-400 EC-IEZ at 1319 (HOA685). Executive visitors were regulars, with Citation 550 EI-PAL & Mitsubishi MU-2 N973BB, but also CL-601 Challenger N46SR at 1205 (from Athens via Le Bourget).

12th October 2002 – With a World Cup qualifying match taking place the following day between England and Slovakia in Bratislava, Air 2000 B.757 G-OOOS (AMM6628) today flew out a plane load of England fans to Bratislava.

23rd October 2002 – Manchester United travelled to Athens for their next match with Olympiakos, on British Midland A.321 G-MIDJ (BMA8905) the previous day. The Greeks once again proved an easy three points for Manchester United, with the Reds winning 3-2 in Athens. This was four straight wins out of four and they had now qualified for the next round.

29th October 2002 – Having already guaranteed their passage into the next stage, United surprisingly slipped up in their away game in Nicosia against Maccabi Haifa, losing 3-0. United again used British Midland for their transportation. A.330 G-WWBD (BMA8907 to Larnaca) was used for the team and Airtours DC-10 G-TAOS (MYT117 to Paphos) took out the fans, both on the 27th. The following day, Air 2000 B.757 G-OOOM (AMM5528 to Larnaca) took more United fans out to Cyprus. The return flights on the 30th October were a little different, with the following flights bringing the fans home: Air 2000 A.320 G-OOAT (AMM6609), A.321 G-OOAF (AMM2275) & B.767-300 G-OOAL (DP053)

13th November 2002 – The final match of the group brought Bayer Leverkusen to Manchester again, arriving on the 12th aboard Condor B.757 D-ABNN (CFG144 from Cologne), which left later for Shannon. Another Condor B.757, D-ABNM, arrived at 1227 (CFG671 from Shannon) on the match day, departing afterwards with the German team. The only two football charters on the day were Aero Lloyd A.321 D-ALAL at 0928 (AEF9930 from Dusseldorf) and A.320 D-ALAF at 0932 (AEF9936 from Cologne), as well as Learjet 60 D-CSIX. The game ended 2-0 to United, which meant they topped the group with 15pts, 6pts ahead of their German rivals, so it was now onwards to the second group phase.

23rd November 2002 – Manchester United's Premier league match today with Newcastle provided some extra flights. Aer Lingus A.330 EI-EWR arrived at 0931 (EIN20C) with 275 Irish United fans; Aer Arran ATR-42 EI-CVS at 0907 (REA4012/3), Hawker 800 EI-RNJ at 1036 and Eastern Airlines Jetstream 41 G-MAJL at 1228 (EZE399 from Manston).

26th November 2002 – Manchester United were now in the second group stage and their recent good form continued with a 3-1 win in Switzerland against FC Basel. British Midland A.321 G-MIDJ (BMA7963) was the team bus, with the fans following in Air 2000 A.320 G-OOAW (AMM3308).

7th December 2002 – Another Premiership game this time against Arsenal, produced numerous visitors, primarily Irish. The Arsenal team arrived the previous day aboard Flightline BAe.146 G-FLTB (FLT591 from Luton). The visitors on match day were Aer Lingus A.330 EI-LAX at 0800 (EIN20C), Aer Arran ATR-72 EI-REA at 0916 (REA4012), Farnair ATR- HB-AFF at 1017 (FAT220), Falcon 2000 HB-IBH, Cessna 421 N421N, Citation 550s EI-PAL & N145DF, Citation 560 G-SIRS, Citation 670 CS-DNF, Hawker 800 EI-RNJ and Learjet 45 G-OLDL.

11th December 2002 – Deportivo La Coruna arrived in Manchester on the 10th aboard Futura B.737-400 EC-GUG at 1128 (FUA7613 from La Coruna), leaving on the 12th. This game did not produce any extra Spanish charters, and just three executive visitors: Citation 550 EI-PAL, Mitsubishi MU-2 N973BB and Hawker 800 CS-DNT (NJE2958 from Dublin).

18th January 2003 – Some of the more crucial Premiership games at Old Trafford this season were attracting much more traffic than had previously been the case, involving teams such as Arsenal, Chelsea and Liverpool. Today, it was the turn of Chelsea which produced many extra arrivals, particularly involving the Irish! There were two Aer Arran flights, ATR-42 EI-CBK at 0908 (REA4044) & ATR-72 EI-REB at 0917 (REA4012) and another Aer Lingus A.330 flight, with EI-LAX at 0740 (EIN20A) carrying 280 fans. Executive visitors were Beech 200 OO-LAC at 0826, Cessna 421 N421N at 0931, PA-34 Seneca N39605 at 0946, Citation 550 EI –PAL at 1041, Hawker 800 EI-RNJ at 1050 and Citation 560 G-REDS at 1113.

9th February 2003 – Today's Manchester derby attracted Aer Arran ATR-72 EI-REB at 0905 (REA4012), Citation 550 CS-DFN at 1027 (NJE8786), BAe.125 EI-RNJ at 1047 and Mitsubishi MU-2 N973BB at 1102.

15th February 2003 – Another big game in the Premiership was today's visit of Arsenal to Manchester United. The Londoners arrived the previous day aboard Flightline BAe.146 G-BPNT (FLT591 from Luton). The match day saw Hawker 800 CS-DNJ at 0906 (NJE3635), Aer Arran ATR-72 EI-REA at 0918 (REA4012), Skynet Airlines B.737-400 EI-CZK at 0931 (SIH1702), BAe.125s EI-WJN at 1011 & EI-RNJ at 1028; Learjet G-OLDR at 1031 and Mitsubishi MU-2 N973BB at 1045.

19th February 2003 – Back to the Champions League now, Juventus were Manchester United's opposition at home on this date. The Italians arrived on Blue Panorama B.737 400 EI-CUN at 1115 (BPA5876 from Turin), and unusually for a group match involving an Italian team, there were some travelling fans! Volare A.321 I-PEKM arrived at 1241 (VLE1806 from Milan) & A.320 I-VLEA at 1303 (VLE1802 from Milan). A couple of Aer Lingus flights were BAe.146s EI-CTN (EIN2210) & EI-CTO (EIN2218). Executive visitors connected with the match included Learjet 55 I-FLYJ, Citations EI-PAL, OY–TKI, & CS-DNW; CL-604 Challenger EI-IRE and Cessna 340 EI-CIJ.

25th February 2003 - United were by now in outstanding form, winning this match 2-0 and a week later went one better, beating Juventus on their own territory 3-0. United this time used British Airways B.757 G-CPEM (BAW9210C) for their flight to Turin. The fans travelled out to Turin on JMC B.757 G-FCLE (JMC703G to Milan), Excel Airways B.737-800 G-XLAA (XLA4228), My Travel A.320 G-YJBM (MYT6731) & A.321 G-CTLA (MYT6743) and Air Scandic A.300 G-TTMC (SCY821). With four wins out of four, Manchester United were now guaranteed to be playing in the knockout stages.

2nd March 2003 – Due to there being no Wembley at the time, the League and FA Cup finals were temporarily held in the new Cardiff Millennium stadium. The teams competing today were Liverpool and of course Manchester United, who travelled down the previous day on BAe.146 G-BLRA (WTN600). Six football charters from Manchester during the morning out to Cardiff were British Airways B.767-300 G-BZHB (BA9212C), Air 2000 B.757 G-OOOC (AMM8852) and JMC A.320s G-BXKB (JMC497G) & G-BXKD (JMC386G); and B.757s G-FCLC (JMC273G) & G-FCLF (JMC691G). Those that travelled were to be disappointed, with the Reds capitulating to their rivals down the M62, losing 2-0.

12th March 2003 – With the other three teams in the group battling for second place in the group, FC Basel certainly had something to play for, in today's match with United. The fans possibly felt that too, as around 3,000 Swiss supporters descended on Manchester. The team arrived on the 18th aboard Swiss MD80 HB-ISX at 1734 (CRX9504), later positioning back to Basle. Match day and the invasion began with Swiss A.321 HB-IOH at 0926 (CRX9494) and they kept coming! Aero Lloyd A.320 D-ALAA at 0939 (AEF9934), Swiss MD80s HB-IUH at 0957 (CRX9500) & HB-IUO at 1348 (CRX9512); Airbus A.330 HB-IQJ at 1431 (CRX9538) and Airbus A.321 HB-IOK at 1502 (CRX9526); Hamburg B.737-700s D-AHID at 1010 (HHI8276) & D-AHIC at 1203 (HHI8264); Neos B.737-800s I-NEOU at 1100 (NOS7330) & I-NEOT at 1356 (NOS7331); Edelweiss A.320 HB-IHX at 1420 (EDW2434 from Zurich), Belair B.757 HB-IHS at 1513 (BHP831), Nordic East MD80 HB-INR at 1542 (NDC900) and Hapag-Lloyd Airbus A.310 D-AHLF at 1551 (HLF3737)! The Irish chartered Aer Arran

ATR-42 EI-BYO (REA4012) and Aer Lingus BAe.146 EI-CLI (EIN2208). Finally, the executive visitors included Citation 550 OE-GPS, Learjet 35 HB-VMB and Citation 560 CS-DFM. The mass support from the Swiss fans clearly seemed to do the trick, with FC Basel earning a credible 1-1 draw. They were collected the following morning by Swiss MD80 HB-IUG (CRX9505).

18th March 2003 - Maybe knowing that they had qualified for the quarter-final stages of the competition, Manchester United this evening took their foot off the gas, being comprehensively beaten away to Deportivo La Coruna, 2-0 for the final group game. The team travelled out on the 17th aboard British Airways Airbus A.320 G-EUUN (BAW9210C to La Coruna), returning on the afternoon of the 19th. There were two fans' charters, My Travel A.320 G-DJAR (MYT6739) & Astraeus B.737-300 G-STRA (AEU877), both to Santiago. However, with 13pts, United still topped the group a clear 6pts ahead of the other three teams. Their first knockout phase match would be with Real Madrid the following month.

8th April 2003 - Manchester United's first leg with Real Madrid would be away from home, with the team travelling out on Azzura Air Airbus A.320 EI-DBC (AZI2160 to Madrid) along with the following fans' flights: Air Scandic A.300s G-SWJW (SCY7711) & G-TTMC (SCY6621); Monarch Airlines A.300 G-MONR (MON9568), British Midland A.321 G-MIDF (BMA7902), Excel Airways B.757 TF-ARD (XLA730), Britannia Airways B.767-300 G-OBYE (BAL884A), Air 2000s B.757 G-OOBD (AMM4478) & G-OOOX (AMM3352) and Astraeus B.737-300 G-STRE (AEU915). A poor performance by the Reds saw them lose 3-1, meaning a mountain to climb for the return leg in two weeks.

23rd April 2003 – Real Madrid arrived on the 22nd aboard Iberia A.340 EC-HDQ (IBE5870), leaving after the match on another A.340, this time EC-ICF (IBE5871). Match day saw an interesting selection of visitors, with Air Europa B.737-800s EC-HBN (AEA435), EC-HJP (AE827) & EC-IDT (AEA801); Spanair MD80 EC-GOM (JKK2677), Skynet B.737-400 EI-CZK (SIH3101 & SIH7023), plus Hawker 800 I-DLOH, Beech 400 I-TOPB, Beech 200 F-GIJB, CL-604 Challengers EI-IRE & N98AG; Falcon 20 EC-EDC, Citations EI-PAL, N312CJ, G-RDBS, D-IFUP, D-CSUN & HB-VNO; Learjets D-CHEF & HB-VJI and BAe.125s G-BJDJ & G-GMAA. There were also a couple of helicopters, with Agusta 109 G-PERI & AS.350 Squirrel G-OHCP, as well as a couple of PA-34 Senecas, G-CTWN (from Southend) & G-HTRL (from Oxford). Finally, a couple of interesting 'bigger' executive visitors were Qatar Amiri Flight A.320 A7-AAG and Roman Abramovich's BBJ P4-GJC arriving from Moscow. All of which witnessed a breath taking 90 minutes worth of football, which saw United lose out 4-3, sending them out of the competition.

27th August 2002 – This fine pair of Tupolev TU-154s making their first visits, were amongst a number of football charters during the day, bringing in some very enthusiastic Zalaegerszeg fans. However, their subsequent fates were not kind. LZ-LCA was withdrawn during 2006 and since scrapped, while LZ-LCS was sold around 2007 as 4K-727 and has been withdrawn since 2011. (Above Denis Norman, below Lee Collins)

27th August 2002 – Malev B.737-400 HA-LEU (MAH1444) seen above making its first visit to Manchester today was one of eight of the airline's B.737's to appear between 1990 - 2006. The airline briefly operated a Manchester-Budapest scheduled service from August 2001 and March 2002. (Denis Norman)

17th September 2002 – Israir Boeing 757 4X-EBM is seen here taxiing in with the Maccabi Haifa team. This aircraft was leased to Israir from 2001 to 2007, and sold in 2011 and is currently stored at Goodyear. (Lee Collins)

17ʰ September 2002 – Turkish airline, Freebird, made their first visit to Manchester today. Established in 2000, they began services on 5ʰ April 2001 with a single MD80 aircraft, TC-MBG. They would go on to operate four MD-80s, until they were sold during 2005. They now operate an all Airbus A.320 fleet. (Lee Collins)

18ʰ September 2002 – A beautiful landing shot of yet another Bulgaria Air Charter TU-154, LZ-LCI, making its first visit. It was bringing in CSKA Sofia for a match with Blackburn Rovers. Operating for Iran Air Tours as EP-MCF, it was written-off at Mashad, Iran, on 1ˢᵗ September 2006, when it caught fire after the nose-wheel collapsed on landing. (Lee Collins)

18ᵗʰ September 2002 – B.737-800 4X-EKI had been leased from North American Airlines earlier in the year, and is seen here still in their basic colours, but with Sun D'or titles. In 2015 it still operates for EL AL, but now sports full new colours. (Nik French)

18ᵗʰ September 2002 – EL AL operated eleven Boeing 757s between 1991 and 2012. 4X-EBT seen here operated for the airline for twenty-one years and was one of their longest-serving Boeing 757s. Note the mass of enthusiasts in the background before the Viewing Park re-opened in its present location. (Lee Collins)

18th September 2002 – Another new Turkish airline to Manchester was Bosphorus European Airways (BEA), with TC-OIM seen here. They began flying in March 2002 with three Airbus A.300s, and for a time they operated a twice-weekly service between Stansted and Istanbul. Today's appearance of TC-OIM was their only visit, and they ceased trading two years later. (Nik French)

18th September 2002 – Arkia B.757 4X-BAZ already had a pedigree by the time of its second visit today! Built in 1988, it had been in before with Air Europe, Air Europa, Caledonian and Istanbul Airlines. In the top right of the picture nose out, is Boeing 757 SE-DUK which was stored at Manchester between 13th August and 23rd October 2002, before eventually re-entering service as G-OOOK. (Nik French)

146

18ᵗʰ September 2002 - A shot from the multi-storey cark park shows three Israeli B.757s, 4X-EBM, 4X-EBT & 4X-BAZ. Also note some of the others of the time, including Ryanair B.737 EI-CJC (in Hertz car rental colour scheme), plus several Air 2000 and Britannia aircraft. (Terry Shone)

30ᵗʰ September 2002 – B.737-400s SX-BLM & SX-BGR became the first Aegean aircraft to appear at Manchester. SX-BLM, which had formerly been in with Axon Airlines, was carrying Olympiakos FC. The following day SX-BGR operated one of three football charters during the day. It is currently the largest Greek airline, calculated by the total number of passengers carried, the number of destinations served and by the fleet size, with 38 Airbus A.319 and A.320 aircraft in service. (Nik French)

30th September 2002 – SX-BGR (Lee Collins)

1st October 2002 – Macedonian Airlines operated three B.737-400s, SX-BMA (seen here), SX-BMB & SX-BMC. The latter two aircraft were regular visitors to Manchester, operating Olympic's twice-weekly service to Athens. SX-BMA was much less common, possibly due to its different seating configuration. (Lee Collins)

1st October 2002 - Hola Airlines B.737-300 EC-IEZ was also drafted in by the Greeks to operate a fans charter for Olympiakos FC. The airline was active between May 2002 and February 2010, and had a regular turnover of second-hand Boeing 737s, seven of which visited Manchester during this period. (Lee Collins)

13th November 2002 – Condor operated a nice little arrangement with two of their Boeing 757s. D-ABNN seen above, arrived with Bayer Leverkusen FC and departed to Shannon over an hour later for maintenance and repaint! (Denis Norman)

13th November 2002 – Condor B.757 D-ABNM positioned in at 1227 (CFG671 from Shannon) to depart after the match with the Bayer Leverkusen team. The aircraft had been having a repaint into the new Thomas Cook colours and titles. (Denis Norman)

18th February 2003 – Blue Panorama made their second visit to Manchester today, with B.737-400 EI-CUN carrying the Juventus team for their match the following evening with Manchester United. Formerly D-AHLS, this aircraft is still operating for the airline, now as I-BPAC. (Nik French)

19th February 2003 – Airbus A.321 I-PEKM, seen here on its first visit was operated by Italian airline, Volare. The first incarnation of this outfit ended in November 2004 when it suspended operations and filed for bankruptcy. The tickets on suspended flights were never refunded to passengers. (Lee Collins)

19th February 2003 – Airbus A.320 I-VLEA seen here in Volareweb colours is still part of the original Volare Group. In May 2006, the airline was re-activated as Volareweb, the re-incarnation of the original Volare airlines. From October 2007 to January 2008, they operated a Manchester–Milan scheduled service, but ceased trading again in October 2009. (Lee Collins)

19th February 2003 – CL-604 Challenger EI-IRE seen here arrived on its first visit in connection with this evening's Manchester United-Juventus match. In December 2011, it was sold as G-CHVN, and is currently registered as C-215 with the Royal Danish Air Force. (Denis Norman)

10th March 2003 – Swiss MD80 HB-ISX arrived at 1734 to drop off FC Basel, before positioning back out to Basle. In 2004, this aircraft was sold to Bulgarian Air Charter as LZ-LDX. (Nik French)

12th March 2003 – The arrival of Swiss A.321 HB-IOH was the first football charter to kick-off a very busy day! In October 2001, due to a number of complicated legal and financial issues, the airline ceased trading and the assets, employees, aircraft and most European routes were transferred to Crossair who were eventually renamed Swiss. Intercontinental routes were taken over on 1st April 2002, officially ending 71 years of Swissair service. (Lee Collins)

12th March 2003 – Aero Lloyd Airbus A.320 D-ALAA was one of two aircraft today from the German airline. After the airline's collapse in 2003, it was sold to America West and is still operating as N602AW, although the airline was taken over by American Airlines in 2013. (Lee Collins)

12th March 2003 – The first of two Hamburg International aircraft arriving today is D-AHID (above) on its first visit. By the time of the second arrival, D-AHIC (below), the sunshine had gone. Just like Volare, the collapse of the original Hamburg Air gave way in July 1998 to a reborn airline, Hamburg International. Employing 215 employees at its peak and wholly owned by its management and venture capitalists, it hit trouble again in 2010, when several charter contracts were revoked. On 19th October 2010 the airline officially went bankrupt. (Both photos Lee Collins)

12th March 2003 – Wearing the colours of the German leisure group, TUI, Italian B.737-800s I-NEOU (above) and I-NEOT (below), both made first visits by Italian airline Neos. Based at Milan-Malpensa, Neos was established in June 2001 as a joint venture between tourism companies Alpitour and TUI. They operate charters flights to destinations in Europe, Russia, Africa, the Middle, Far East, Caribbean, Mexico and Brazil. They currently operate six B.737-800s and three B.767-300s. (Both photos Lee Collins)

12th March 2003 – Seen seconds from touchdown, MD80 HB-IUO was just a small part of the Swiss invasion. It had visited earlier in the day, operating Crossair's early morning Basle flight instead of their regular Saab 2000. This aircraft was sold to Viking Airlines as SE-RDE in May 2003, and is now operating with Khors Air as UR-CJE. (Lee Collins)

12th March 2003 – Even German airline Hapag-Lloyd was involved in today's airlift! Seen in a rather smart livery, is A.310 D-AHLZ on its first visit to Manchester. Originally established in 1972, Hapag-Lloyd became part of the TUI group in 1997 and by January 2007 was fully merged into TUI and operating as TUIfly. (Lee Collins)

12th March 2003 – MD80 HB-IUH formerly carried the gaudy red colours and McDonald's titles, before being repainted into standard Crossair colours in early 2000. Sold as TC-FLO in 2005, it is currently operating for Kish Air as EP-LCO. (Lee Collins)

12th March 2003 – Another new airline to Manchester was the arrival of Edelweiss Airbus A.320 HB-IHX. Owned by Swiss International and the Lufthansa group, flights began in October 1995 using a single MD80. In 2015, they operate a mix of A.320 & A.330s for both European and Intercontinental destinations. (Nik French)

12th March 2003 – Arguably the pick of today's football flights was the first visit of a Swiss Airbus A.330-200, with the arrival of HB-IQJ. Only one further Swiss A.330 has visited Manchester to date, this being HB-IQA on 2nd September 2011. The airline's fleet of A.300-200s would eventually be superseded by the A.330-300s. (Lee Collins)

12th March 2003 – Yet another airline no longer in existence is Nordic Airlink. MD80 HB-INR is seen here, having recently arrived from Basle. Between 1996 and 2007, the airline operated scheduled and charter services within Scandinavia and Europe. It was bought by Norwegian Air Shuttle in 2007 and became fully integrated the following year. (Nik French)

12th March 2003 – Still wearing Swissair tail colours, A.321 HB-IOK (CRX9526/7 f/t Zurich) was delivered new in March 1999, and still operates for Swiss. (Nik French)

12th March 2003 – Aer Arran increased their presence at Manchester during the year. Initially operating football charters from Dublin, in June 2003 they began schedule flights to Galway. Here, ATR-42 EI-BYO is on short finals on a charter from Dublin. (Nik French)

12th March 2003 – Above, Boeing 757 HB-IHS is making its first visit today for Belair, who have a long and complicated history. Originally formed in 1952 as Balair, they operated for the next forty years as a charter airline, building their fleet from Vickers Vikings up to Douglas DC-10s. In 1993 Balair merged with another Swiss operator, CTA, and formed closer ties with Swissair. Balair folded in 2001, following the grounding of Swissair, but within months was it was reformed as Belair. In 2015, they form part of the very successful Air Berlin group. Below, an early afternoon shot of the football related aircraft parked on T2. (Both photos Nik French)

22nd April 2003 – The first of two Iberia A.340s on consecutive days was EC-HDQ, arriving today with the Real Madrid team. The second aircraft, EC-ICF, arrived the following evening to return the team back to Madrid. (Denis Norman)

23rd April 2003 – EC-IDT was one of three Air Europe B.737-800s on the day, bringing in Real Madrid fans, and looking very smart with its winglets! (Lee Collins)

23rd April 2003 – Skynet B.737-400 EI-CZK made its first visit in February 2003. This short-lived Irish airline was formed with commercial help from Aeroflot, and began a Shannon-Amsterdam-Moscow service in June 2001. With the addition of a second Boeing 737, it was planned to add Warsaw, Vienna and Brussels to their network, but this was never executed. Their end came in May 2004, when operations were suspended due to spiralling debts. (Lee Collins)

23rd April 2003 – Amiri Royal Flight Airbus A.320 A7-AAG is seen in full Qatar Airways colours, as are all Royal flight aircraft. It was making its first visit, bringing in a number of VIPs for the Manchester United-Real Madrid match. Co-incidentally, the airline had just introduced a four-times-weekly Manchester-Doha service earlier in the month. (Lee Collins)

23rd April 2003 – Boeing 737-7CG (BBJ) P4-GJC owned by Russian billionaire Roman Abramovich brought in the man himself, plus two other passengers for the Man U-Real Madrid game. In June 2003, he became the proud owner of Chelsea FC. (Lee Collins)

23rd April 2003 – BAe.125-700 G-BJDJ is seen here, having recently arrived from Dublin. Registered new in 1981, it made its first visit to Manchester in September 1983, and operated for various UK operators over the next twenty-three years. It is currently registered as RA-02802. (Denis Norman)

23rd April 2003 – One of the numerous executive visitors also dropping in this vital match was Beech 200 Super King Air F-GIJB. Twelve years later, it is still current on the French register. (Denis Norman)

23rd April 2003 – Amsterdam-based Citation 560 D-CSUN (GZA2133 from Eindhoven) made its only visit to Manchester today. It was German-registered throughout its time with Excellent Air (2001-2006), but in early 2007 it was sold to Solid Air as PH-ILA. (Denis Norman)

23rd April 2003 – Another BAe.125 visiting for the Manchester United-Real Madrid match is Hawker 800 D-CHEF, having recently arrived from Cologne. It had made its first visit to Manchester on 24th April 2002, and was sold in May 2009. (Denis Norman)

24th April 2003 – Smart-looking Learjet 31, HB-VJI (FPG961), is seen departing for Paris-Le Bourget having night-stopped. Newly delivered in 1989 it made its first visit to Manchester in April 1991 and is now based in Germany as D-CFST. (Denis Norman)

24th April 2003 – CL-604 Challenger N98AG, registered from November 2002 until January 2007, was also making its only visit to Manchester. It is seen here leaving for Luton, having arrived the previous afternoon from Stansted. (Denis Norman)

CHAMPIONS LEAGUE FINAL
28ᵗʰ May 2003

Manchester United had made a bid to host the UEFA Champions League final back in 1998, as these things were decided well in advance. The decision day came during November 2001 and Manchester was successful. Even though Wembley had been in the running, the Manchester bid may well have failed, as any major European competitions being played in England would have almost certainly taken place at Wembley. Fortunately for Manchester, Wembley was being completely rebuilt and out of the running.

The final in May would take place between two Italian teams, Juventus and AC Milan, so from an enthusiast's perspective; it was no bad thing that Manchester United got knocked out in the quarter finals, as it would have been a disaster if two English teams took part!

The organisation and planning by the airport for the Final needed close co-operation between a vast number of companies and organisations, with many remaining sceptical about the practicalities. One of the various challenges was not knowing who the two finalists would be until after the semi finals, just two weeks before the final. The Champions League which began in September included three English and two Scottish teams. Any planning had to take into account that two teams from within the UK could be involved. However, it was likely that the two competing teams would be from abroad, along with their attendant fans.

The Manchester bid was backed by Manchester City Council, Manchester United, the Football Association and the UK government, as well as the airport. Having good facilities was an integral part of the bid. A multi-terminal airport would help to separate rival fans, and a two-runway airport would provide the capacity and a backup if one runway was disabled for any reason. There was also plenty of hotel accommodation, although most fans were expected to make day trips. In any case, Manchester Airport was used to handling football flights, and not only from visiting European fans. They also coped with Manchester United travelling away and mass 'getaways' such as the Champions League Final in 1999.

Some airport personnel were sent to Scotland to train for the final in May 2002. Glasgow and Prestwick airports were used, as they were not 'slot-controlled'. To cover themselves the airlines told the handling agents they would use both airports for the same flights, so pre-planning was difficult. To make matters worse, some fans were confused as to which airport they had arrived at, and used the wrong buses after the match.

Slots were issued and new capacity limits were agreed for the day. Runway 24L was kept open all day, although its operation was restricted due to the number of aircraft parked at the eastern end. The airport also had their regular traffic to look after, and keep any inconvenience to the absolute minimum. Their existing operators were concerned that their operations may be at the mercy of these extra flights, as the airport would be tempted by the extra revenue these flights would generate.

Real Madrid knocked Manchester United out of the competition, so the entire fleet of Spanair and Futura booked slots, even though they still had to overcome Juventus in the semi-final first! As a result, these slots were held on a provisional basis. The only slots given full status were sponsors' flights, such as the Dutchbird Boeing 757 (PH-DBH) for Amstel, which made its booking in January! Slot confirmation would only be given after the semi-final had produced the finalists. Surprisingly, Juventus were knocked out, and Real Madrid and AC Milan beat their local rivals Inter Milan. This pairing guaranteed Manchester Airport was going to have a busy day on the 28th May, as it's a long journey by road from Italy to Manchester! UEFA had previously informed the airport to plan on around 200 aircraft, including executives, and they weren't far off the mark!

Various cross airport teams were at work, and had been from some months. Airfield operations, terminal operations, ground transport, emergency procedures etc had to co-ordinate and work together. The airport planning team had to try and work out where to park everything. Every day saw more flights asking for slots, whilst others were constantly changing their schedules. The worst of these was Eurofly, who resubmitted their programme in the last 24 hours, and then changed it again once the aircraft had arrived!

The first arrival connected with the match was on the 26th May when Volare A.330 I-VLEH (VLE1882 from Milan-Malpensa) arrived at 1656 with the AC Milan Team and entourage. Later that evening, the Juventus team arrived on Blue Panorama B.737-400 at 1841 (BPA5852 from Turin). When it was all over on the 29th May, with the departure of Eurofly A.320 at 2306 (EEZ1991 to Verona), there had been 469 extra movements connected with the match:

May 2003	Arrive	Depart	Total
Monday 26th	4	3	7
Tuesday 27th	10	7	17
Wednesday 28th	181	56	237
Thursday 29th	41	169	210

It was inevitable that ATC records would be broken sometime within the four-day period. The previous record of 706 movements in a calendar day was shattered when 889 movements were handled on the 28th. Even the 29th saw 845 movements. If you look at the 24-hour period (0700-0659 28th-29th local time), the figure was 942! This comprised of 488 arrivals and 454 departures. The busiest arrival hour was 1800-1859 on the 28th, with 41 arrivals. The busiest departure hour in this 24 hour period was shared by the 0700-0759 and 0800-0859 hour on the 28th, with 33 departures within each hour. The busiest hour for departures during the four days (26th-29th) was on the 29th with 35 from 0900-0959. During the huge arrival surge on the 28th, there was no airborne holding until after 1600, when there was a delay of around 20 minutes.

Official figures said there were 55,000 extra passengers over the four days. To help them get to and from Old Trafford, 800-plus coaches were used from all over the UK. There were also plenty of enthusiasts from the UK and Europe. Reportedly at least one 'spotter' from the USA had arrived on the Continental flight from Newark on the 28th.

An estimated 7,000 enthusiasts appeared, many of which were gathered in the specially enlarged Viewing Park. Precautions, such as restricting the number of cars on the top level of the T1 multi-storey car park, had to be taken to ensure the viewing area there did not collapse under the weight of people! Lots of enthusiasts from London were seen to be well equipped against Manchester's famous rain. However, although the weather was grim to begin with, by late morning it had blown away, giving way to a warm and sunny afternoon, which was perfect for the thousands of photographers.

It wasn't just enthusiasts that the airport had to deal with, it was also sponsors, VIPs, royalty, presidents, prime ministers, government officials, celebrities, UEFA senior officials, media and local communities, who all had to be looked after. To deal with all of this, extra staff were drafted in and 500 airport staff worked extra shifts.

Terminals 1 & 3 were allocated to Juventus with AC Milan in T2. Having been bussed in from the airport to the ground, coaches were numbered and parked at opposite ends of the ground. Fans were told to return to the same coach number in the same location, which worked reasonably well. These coaches would return to the airport, with T1 & T3-bound coaches travelling down Ringway Road, past the Airport Hotel to hold. The T2-bound coaches were to exit at the M56/cargo centre junction and hold at a point on the old T2 haul road. The idea of the holding points was to prevent passenger overload at the terminals, by controlling the flow. Incidentally, some flights were shared with both AC Milan and Juventus fans on the same aircraft.

Despite the coach drivers being briefed on the inbound routings, which were also signed around the airport, many went to the terminals directly, particularly T2. This meant the police had to close the building for a time. Several drivers chose to ignore the police directions by dropping off their passengers. As coach drivers are restricted by EU regulations regarding their hours of work, at least one driver was known to have dropped off his passengers at the cargo centre. He was unable to wait as he had to ferry back to his offices before his hours ran out! Before driving away he told his bewildered passengers "It's OK, it's only a mile away over there"!

T1 became very congested as well, with the police adopting crowd control tactics. Megaphone announcements were made in Italian by some of the many language students brought in for the day. There was plenty of shouting and jeering, even from the losing fans, but there was no violence. Most passengers were without bags, and as they had been checked through already, they had boarding cards for their return flight. However, there were some problems caused by the ground staff at some of the Italian airports, who had pulled the wrong boarding card. This meant that the passengers had a valid card for the inbound flight only when going through security, and not for the return!

With the late finish, due to crew-hours Futura delayed some of their new departures, but other flights were delayed for other reasons – such as having no flight crew! A Eurofly crew was noted wandering around T1 at 0400, looking for the crew check-in which had long since closed! From the schedule, they were due to take a flight out of T2 at 0300! Apparently, they were late because they went to the match and ended up stuck on a coach when they should have been resting. The congestion and late finish resulted in large number of fans funnelling into the T1 security control at the same time as regular passengers appearing for the first normal flights of the day.

Airport operations had been busy working out where were to park the extra aircraft. Firstly, they had to find out which team the flights were for, so all slot requests had to contain this information, which was anything but straight forward! Eurofly had an aircraft coming in with Juventus fans, but was taking AC Milan fans back, while Neos had the reverse. There were the shared fights too, with Monarch from Naples, Britannia from Pisa and Nordic East from Basle; as well as both Austrian Airlines flights (A.321 OE-LBA & A.340 OE-LAK from Bari and Pescara). Every available space was required, and then some! It was decided that aircraft with GPU and their own airstairs (such as MD80s/737/BAE.146/RJs) could park on the south side/R24L taxiway network, whilst keeping 24L operational with a limited taxiway layout and a shortened length. If the airport had been on easterlies, this might have proved trickier.

To minimise runway crossings, passengers from these flights would be taken straight from the aircraft to Old Trafford, with the control authorities setting up operations at the R24L Fire Station. This was one part of the operation that did not go as well as it could have. There were communication difficulties with the coach controllers, which caused delays. Some of the other delays were caused by aircraft charterers not organising coaches, and leaving the passengers to their own devices on arrival at the terminal! All the necessary service vehicles going to south side would use the internal perimeter road, which was designated one way. However, due to unfamiliarity with its layout, a catering vehicle strayed onto the runway just as a Brussels Airlines A.319 landed, causing an Azzura B.737-700 to overshoot!

Back on the main apron, double parking or even more was required once the aircraft had been handled. To make more space, stored aircraft Monarch DC-10 G-DMCA, white B.757 PH-ITA and the two FLS A.320s G-JDFW & OY-CNB were all towed down to the holding loop at the west end of R24L. Just to complicate matters, Dragonair B.747 B-KAB, which arrived on 26th went tech out, and required an engine change. The airline rightly refused to move their aircraft down there, as the engine was being changed by a gang of engineers flown in especially from Hong Kong and it was just impractical to move it. In fact, there was an idea that all the freighters due on the 28th (Dragonair, Cathay Pacific, China Airlines, Cargolux) should go elsewhere as Wednesday was the day with the most B.747 freighters arriving, but sensibly this was not followed through. The stand parking plans were changed right up to the first arrival, not helped by the airlines changing plans! Every available piece of kit was pressed into action. Extra equipment was brought in by some agents, with the airport ending up with 400 extra chocks! Bizjet and executive aircraft were parked in and around the NEA complex, and use was also made of the engine-test bay.

By 2300, it is believed that 202 aircraft were parked on the airfield, although this figure probably did not include the residents of the engineering and general aviation hangars. The theory had been to leave some of the football flights on terminal pier-served stands, which would be gone in the early hours, so the first regular outbounds could be towed on to the piers. More night-stoppers were parked on the taxiway centreline around the horseshoe, the area between Pier B and T3. In the event of delays or whatever, some of these outbounds were dispatched from their parking areas.

The first departure after the match was the Global Express EC-IBD at 2306. By midnight, 21 executive flights had departed, which formed a nice queue as the airport was operating on single runway operations. The first airliner to depart was Dutchbird B.757 PH-DBH at 0116 (DBR9326 to Amsterdam).

Below is a complete listing of all Champions League Final-related aircraft visiting over the four-day period:

AIRLINERS

C-

Skyservice	A.330	C-FRAV

CS-

Air Luxor	A.320	CS-TMW / TNB

D-

Cirrus	Dash-8	D-BKIM
Gandalf Aw	Do.328	D-BGAG
LTU	A.320	D-ALTD
	A.321	D-ALSA
	A.330	D-ALPE

EC-

Futura	B.737s	EC-GNZ / EC-GRX / EC-HHH / EC-IHI / EC-INP / N254RY
LTE	B.757s	EC-HQX / HRB
Spanair	MD80	EC-GCV / GGV / GQG / GOU
Travel Service	B.737	EC-ILX

F-

Air Mediterranee	A.321	F-GYAN / GYAO
Star Europe	A.320	F-GRSD / GRSG / GRSH
	A.330	F-GRSQ

G-

Air Scandic	A.300	G-SWJW / TTMC
Britannia	B.757	G-BYAE
	B.767	G-BNYS / OBYD / OBYG
Eastern Aw	Jetstream	G-CBDA
Monarch	A.300	G-MONR / MONS
	B.757	G-DAJB

HB-

Nordic East	MD80	HB-INR
Swiss	A.321	HB-IOI

I-

Air Dolomiti	CRJ	I-ADJA
Air Europe Italy	B.767	I-VIMQ
Air One	B.737	EI-CXJ

Alitalia	B.767	EI-CRF / CRO / I-DEIL
	MD11s	I-DUPD / DUPE
	MD80s	I-DACU / DATP / DAVA
Azzura Air	A.320	EI-DBC / DBD
	RJ-85	EI-CNI / CNJ / CNK
	B.737s	D-AGEY / AGEZ / EI-CXE
Blue Panorama	B.737s	EI-CUA / CUD / CUN
Eurofly	A.320s	I-BIKC / BIKD / BIKF / EEZC / EEZD / EEZE /
	EEZF / EEZG	
Neos	B.737s	I-NEOS / NEOT / NEOU
Volare	A.320s	F-OHFR / F-OHFT / I-PEKQ
	A.321s	I-PEKM / PEKN
	A.330	I-VLEC / VLEE / VLEH

OE-
| Austrian Airlines | A.321 | OE-LBA |
| | A.340 | OE-LAK |

OH-
| Finnair | B.757 | OH-LBR |

OY-
| Premiair | A.330 | OY-VKH / VKI |

PH-
Dutchbird	B.757	PH-DBH
KLM	Fk-50	PH-KVG
	Fk-70	PH-KZH
KLM Excel	EMB-145	PH-RXC
Transavia	B.737s	PH-HZB / HZG / HZI

SE-
| Viking | MD80 | SE-RDF |

TF-
| Air Atlanta | B.747 | TF-ATD |

9A-
| Air Adriatic | MD80 | 9A-CBD |

9H-
| Air Malta | B.737 | 9H-ADH |

5Y-
| East African | B.767 | 5Y-QQQ |

EXECUTIVE
C-
| Global Express | C-GJTK | |

CS-
Citation 550	CS-DHA / DHB
Citation 560	CS-DNW
Falcon 2000	CS-DNR / DNS

D-

Beech 1900	D-CBSF
Cessna 421	D-INTA
Metro	D-CSWF
PA-42	D-IHLA

EC-

Global Express	EC-IBD

EI-

Learjet	EI-IAW

F-

Beech 1900	F-HCHA
Citation 550	F-GJYD
EMB-120	F-GVBR
Falcon 50	F-GMOT

G-

BAe.125s	G-IFTE / OLDD
Beech 200	G-BYCP
Citation 550	G-SPUR
Citation 560	G-NETA
Metro	G-BUKA

HB-

PA-60	HB-LIN
Citation 525	HB-VNL / VNO
Citation 560	HB-VNH
CL-601	HB-ILK / IVS
Falcon 20	HB-VJV
Falcon 2000	HB-IAZ / IBH

I-

BAe.125	I-CIGH
Beech 400	I-PIZ / TOPB / TOP / VITH
Citation 525	I-DEUM
Citation 550	I-FJTB / FJTC / JESO / MTVB
Falcon 10	I-CREM
Falcon 20	I-GOBJ
Falcon 50	I-SNAB
Falcon 900	I-TLCM
Falcon 2000	I-SNAW
Hawker 800	I-ALHO / DLOH / RONY
Gulf 4	I-LUBI
Gulf 5	I-DEAS
Learjet	I-ERJC / ERJD / VULC / ZOOM
Metro	I-VICY
P.180 Avanti	I-BCOM

LX-
Learjet   LX-DSL / OMC / PAT / PRA
N
Citation 525   N158CJ
Global Express   N700HX
OE-
CL-604   OE-IYA
OO-
Learjet   OO-LFV
PH-
Metro   PH-DYM
P4-
BBJ   P4-GJC
S5-
Citation 550   S5-BAX
TC-
Falcon 900   TC-AKK
VP-
CL-601   VP-CBS

There were also two military movements, with Italian Air Force A.319CJ MM62174 (28th) & Falcon 900EX MM62171 (29th) and 93 airliners of 18 different basic types from 18 countries with 34 airlines involved.

Aircraft in interesting liveries were B.767-300 I-VIMQ in Air Europe colours but operating a Volare flight. Volare A.320s F-OHFR & I-PEKQ were in Volareweb colours, Lauda Air Italy sub-chartered East African B.767-300 5Y-QQQ and LTU A.320 D-ALTD was in Hertha BSC Berlin colours. The Skyservice A.330, C-FRAV, was in basic Khalifa colours and no titles, and some all white aircraft were KLM Excel EMB-145 PH-RXC, BIE A.321 F-GYAO arriving with an Air Mediterranee call sign but departing with a Blue Line call sign. Meanwhile another BIE A.321, F-GYAN, did exactly the opposite! A couple of Meridiana MD-80s were coming and then didn't, although one went into Liverpool, which took about 15 aircraft, mostly bizjets that did not come to Manchester although they had slots.

In fact the biz/general aviation requests were constantly changing. There were 69 GA aircraft involved from 17 countries with 19 different bizjet types, and 9 turboprop types. If you look at the slot request from the night before, there were several no-shows which are detailed below, although some of these went to Liverpool:

CL604   OY-CLD
Falcon 2000   CS-DFC, CS-DFD, HB-IAY
Falcon 900   HB-IBG, I-FLYW, LX-GJL
Falcon 50   I-CAFD, I-ULJA
Falcon 20   I-FLYP

Falcon 10	I-FJDC
Learjet	LX RPL, I-AIRW
Citations	CS-DHC, CS-DNZ, D-CFUW, D-IJYP, EC-IAB, F-GTRY, HB-VMY,
	I-ALKA, I-DAGF, I-LEAL, I-LVNB, OY-LLA
HS.125	EI-RNI
Astra	EC GDL
Metro	F-GPSN,
Beech 200	I-PIAH

The following is a list of the VIP/sponsors flights:
Global Express EC-IBD – Juventus VIPs
Beech 1900 F-HCHA – Coca Coca/RTL
Dutchbird B.757 PH-DBI I/Star Europe A.320 FGRSD - Amstel
CL601 Challenger HB-ILK/Falcon 20 HB-VJV - UEFA (VJV had Phil Collins, the well-known
UEFA official onboard!)
KLM Fokker 50 PH-KVG - Heineken
KLM Fokker 70 PH-KZH – Mastercard
Spanair MD80 EC-GOU – Juventus VIPs
Volare A.330 I-VLEC – AC Milan VIPs
Blue Panorama B.737s EI-CUA/CUD/CUN - Juventus VIPs
Gandalf Do328 D-BGAG – also carried VIPs.

In the end, there were no arrests in Manchester, just a huge carnival atmosphere and good weather. Some Italian press reports were critical of the airport, but under the circumstances it was always going to be impossible for things to run totally smooth. The organisation whose comments really mattered were when UEFA said that the Manchester final was "the best ever"!

PHOTO GALLERY 28th MAY 2003

Here is a fantastic selection of visitors over the four-day period of late May 2003, which seems unlikely ever to be repeated.

Ground Views

Volare Airbus A.321 I-PEKM (Nik French)

LTU Airbus A.330 D-ALPE (Lloyd Robinson)

East African B.767-300 5Y-QQQ (Lloyd Robinson)

Dutchbird Boeing 757 PH-DBH (Glenn Wheeler)

Travel Service B.737-800 EC-ILX. (Stuart Prince)

Futura B.737-800 EC-INP (Stuart Prince)

Blue Panorama B.737-400 EI-CUN (Stuart Prince)

Skyservice Airbus A.330 C-FRAV (Stuart Prince)

Austrian Airlines A.340 OE-LAK (Stuart Prince)

LTU Airbus A.320 D-ALTD (Nik French)

Alitalia Boeing 767-300 EI-CRF (Allan Jones)

Star Europe Airbus A.300 F-GRSQ (Nik French)

Air Europe Italy I-VIMQ Boeing 767-300 I-VIMQ (Nik French)

Alitalia MD80 I-DAVA (Lloyd Robinson)

Alitalia MD11 I-DUPE. (Nik French)

Volareweb Airbus A.320 I-VLEA (Nik French)

Volare Airbus A.300 I-VLEH (Nik French)

Italian Air Force Airbus A.319CJ MM62174 (Nik French)

Neos Boeing 737-800 I-NEOT (Lloyd Robinson)

Alitalia Boeing 767-300 I-DEIL (Lloyd Robinson)

Alitalia Boeing 767-300 I-DEIL (Lloyd Robinson)

Spanair MD80 EC-GGV (Lloyd Robinson)

Spanair MD80 EC-GGV (Lloyd Robinson)

Air Adriatic MD80 9A-CBD (Lloyd Robinson)

Transavia B.737-800 PH-HZB (Lloyd Robinson)

Air One B.737-400 EI-CXJ (Glenn Wheeler)

KLM Cityhopper Fokker 70 PH-KZH (Glenn Wheeler)

LTU Airbus A.321 D-ALSA & LTE Boeing 757 EC-HRB (Lloyd Robinson)

Italian fans embarking from Austrian A.340 OE-LAK
(Lloyd Robinson)

Volare Airbus A.330 I-VLEC is seen bringing in yet another plane load of AC Milan fans. (Both photos Lloyd Robinson)

(Both photos Lloyd Robinson)

(Both photos Lloyd Robinson)

(Paul Rowland)

Some of the thousands of spotters on the viewing park (Lloyd Robinson)

194

Spectators and Alitalia MD11 I-DUPE passing the viewing park. (Both photos Rick Ward)

Falcon 900 TC-AKK (Lloyd Robinson)

Gulfstream 5 I-DEAS (Lloyd Robinson)

Beech 1900 D-CBSF (Nik French)

Cessna 525 Citation Jet HB-VNL (Lloyd Robinson)

Gandalf Airways Do.328JET D-BGAG (Rick Ward)

Falcon 20 HB-VJV (Lloyd Robinson)

Learjet 35 I-VULC (Lloyd Robinson)

Falcon 50 F-GMOT (Lloyd Robinson)

Gulfstream 4 I-LUBI (Stuart Prince)

Learjet 45 LX-DSL (Lloyd Robinson)

Metroliner I-VICY (Lloyd Robinson)

Global Express EC-IBD (Lloyd Robinson)

Citation 550 G-SPUR (Lloyd Robinson)

Global Express N700HX (Lloyd Robinson)

Beech 200 Super King Air G-BYCP (Glenn Wheeler)

Hawker 800 I-RONY (Lloyd Robinson)

BAE.125-700 I-CIGH (Lloyd Robinson)

Learjet 60 LX-PRA (Lloyd Robinson)

CL-604 Challenger OE-IYA (Lloyd Robinson)

Falcon 10 I-CREM (Lloyd Robinson)

Global Express C-GJTK (Lloyd Robinson)

Piaggio P.180 Avanti I-BCOM (Lloyd Robinson)

Beech 1900 F-HCHA (Nik French)

Hawker 800 I-DLOH (Lloyd Robinson)

Beech 400 I-IPIZ (Lloyd Robinson)

CL-601 Challenger VP-CBS (Lloyd Robinson)

Falcon 2000 HB-IBH (Lloyd Robinson)

Falcon 900 I-TLCM (Lloyd Robinson)

Piaggio P.180 Avanti I-FXRC (Nik French)

Roman Abramovich's BBJ P4-GJC (Glenn Wheeler)

(Nik French)

(Lloyd Robinson)

(Both photos Lloyd Robinson)

(Stuart Prince)

CL-604 Challenger OE-IYA (Glenn Wheeler)

Air Luxor Airbus A.320 OY-CNB (Glenn Wheeler)

Cirrus Airlines Dash-8 D-BKIM (Glenn Wheeler)

Austrian Airlines A.340 OE-LAK (Glenn Wheeler)

(Glenn Wheeler)

(Both photos Glenn Wheeler)

Star Europe A.320 F-GRSD (Glenn Wheeler)

Air Dolomiti CRJ I-ADJA (Glenn Wheeler)

Futura B.737-400 N254RY (Glen Wheeler)

Eurofly A.320 I-BIKD (Glenn Wheeler)

(Glenn Wheeler)

(Both photos Glenn Wheeler)

(Both photos Glenn Wheeler)

(Both photos Glenn Wheeler)

(Both photos Glenn Wheeler)

(Both photos Glenn Wheeler)

(Glenn Wheeler)

(Lloyd Robinson)

225

Tower Views

(Both photos Lloyd Robinson)

(Both photos Lloyd Robinson)

(Both photos Lloyd Robinson)

(Both photos Lloyd Robinson)

229

(Both photos Lloyd Robinson)

(Both photos Glenn Wheeler)

(Both photos Glenn Wheeler)

(Both photos Glenn Wheeler)

(Both photos Glenn Wheeler)

(Glenn Wheeler)

(Both photos Glenn Wheeler)

(Both photos Glenn Wheeler)

(Both photos Glenn Wheeler)

(Glenn Wheeler)

(Glenn Wheeler)

(Glenn Wheeler)

(Both photos Glenn Wheeler)

(Both photos Glenn Wheeler)

(Glenn Wheeler)

(Glenn Wheeler)

245

(Glenn Wheeler)

(Both photos Glenn Wheeler)

(Both photos Glenn Wheeler)

(Both photos Glenn Wheeler)

249

29th May 2003 – Unfortunately the final the previous evening did not live up to the hype. The immoval force against the impenetrable object just ground out the 90 minutes to the ultimate conclusion, extra time and then penalties. Both Juventus and AC Milan struggled with spot icks as well, but AC Milan finally came out on top, winning 3-2 on penalties. Volare A.330 I-VLEE (EEZ1863 to Milan Malpensa) is seen here with the AC Milan team and officials boarding for their flight home. (Nik French)

RINGWAY PUBLICATIONS

BOOKS PUBLISHED:

SIXTIES & SEVENTIES DIVERSION DAYS

SIXTIES RINGWAY 1960 – 1969

SEVENTIES RINGWAY 1970 – 1979

EIGHTIES RINGWAY 1980 – 1984

EIGHTIES RINGWAY 1985 – 1989

WOODFORD IN PICTURES

MANCHESTER AIRPORT 75TH ANNIVERSARY 1938 - 2013

Coming next:

EIGHTIES DIVERSION DAYS

Forthcoming:

NINETIES RINGWAY

CLASSIC JETS

CLASSIC PROPS

NINETIES DIVERSIONS

MANCHESTER AIRPORT FOOTBALL TRAFFIC VOL.2

Our books can be purchased from our on-line shop,
through our stockists
or by ordering from any good bookshop.

MANCHESTER MOVEMENT
DATA CDs

50 YEARS OF DIVERSIONS MANCHESTER AIRPORT 1960 – 2010

SIXTIES MOVEMENTS

SEVENTIES MOVEMENTS

EIGHTIES MOVEMENTS

NINETIES MOVEMENTS

NOUGHTIES MOVEMENTS

SEVENTIES ATC AUDIO CD, VOL 1

Coming next:

SEVENTIES ATC AUDIO CD, VOL 2

*Our CDs can be purchased from our online shop
or from the two Aviation Shops (TAS)
at Manchester Airport*

Visit our historic website coverings all aspects of Manchester Airport:
www.ringwaypublications.com

We can be contacted via our website contact page or by emailing:
info@ringwaypublications.com